DRY STONE WALLING

vii
ited
WC1
by the
Drystane
nlxxii
n by
td

Two Galloway dykers repairing a 4 foot 6 inch open dyke. The artist. Mason Trotter, RSA, has not shown the guiding strings. Isle of Man in the far distance.

The Author's two-year-old great-grandson Neil

First published in mcm
by Faber and Faber Lin
24 Russell Square London
Second Edition published
Stewartry of Kirkcudbright
Dyking Committee in mc
Printed in Great Britai
Grieve the Printers L
Dumfries

FOREWORD

When the book *Dry Stone Walling* by the late Colonel Rainsford-Hannay went out of print it was the unanimous wish of the Stewartry Drystane Dyking Committee, which he founded in 1938, that it should be reprinted.

This has been made possible by the generosity of his widow, Mrs. Rainsford-Hannay, who has lent us the necessary money.

We have had the greatest encouragement from the whole Rainsford-Hannay family even to the fourth generation, as exemplified by the photos of Colonel and Mrs. Rainsford-Hannay's two year-old great-grandson Neil busily dyking!

After Colonel Rainsford-Hannay's death I was asked to take over the Convenership of the Drystane Dyking Committee: this I did in 1961 and with the sterling help of a most energetic Committee and of many other enthusiasts, we have followed Colonel Rainsford-Hannay's example by holding Competitions in our home area, and of initiating Training Courses. We have also just completed an instructional Film Strip.

Though Dry Stone Dyking is fortunately at present no longer a dying Craft it is essential that those concerned should maintain their interest, for we work on a shoe string and are entirely dependent on the support and interest of our friends.

In 1968 we formed a Dry Stone Walling Association through which medium we make contacts in all parts of the country, and thus try to keep those interested in touch with each other.

We hope that you will derive as much pleasure and information from Colonel Rainsford-Hannay's book as we have.

1

There has been no revisal, for we feel it is too well written to admit alteration, but we have added an addendum as to up-to-date figures and information.

ELIZABETH MURRAY USHER
Convener
Stewartry Drystane Dyking Committee

Cally Estate Office
Gatehouse-of-Fleet
Scotland
April 1972

ADDENDUM

Costs (with reference to page 43)

Estimates for similar lengths of Fencing and Dyking quoted for in Galloway in 1971 are:

100 yards 5 plain and 1 barb wire fence—cost of supply and erection—£41·00.

100 yards Rylock woven wire fence + 1 plain and 1 barb—cost of supply and erection—£51·00.

100 yards Dry Stone Dyke—£100·00.

The initial difference in price is at first sight alarming but, of course, Dry Stone Dykes last for ever.

Grants

Agricultural Grants are available. These vary from time to time but information is obtainable from the Department of Agriculture. Work must not in any case commence before an Application for Grant is approved.

Demonstrations

Demonstrations have been held of recent date at the Royal Show, the Royal Highland Show, the Great Yorkshire Show, and at Bakewell Show, Derbyshire, and at Moreton-in-Marsh Show, Gloucestershire.

Competitions

The Stewartry Drystane Dyking Committee held their 16th Competition at Gatehouse-of-Fleet in September 1971 (the first Competition being held in October 1939) with over 40 entries from Scotland and the North of England.

Competitions are held also at Washburn Valley Farmers' Show, Blubberhouses, nr. Harrogate; Malhamdale Show, Settle; Upper Wharfedale Agricultural Society, Kilnsey, Yorkshire; at Matlock, Derbyshire and, until recently, also at Farleton Ploughing, Hedging and Walling Competition, nr. Kendal, Westmorland.

Training Courses

The original Training Courses organis⊖
ford Hannay were held in 1948 and 1950 – –

In 1968 Training Courses were resum⊙
Gatehouse-of-Fleet under the joint auspi·
A.H.F.I.T.B. and the Education Authorit

Since then several Courses have been he
Kirkcudbright, Dumfriesshire, Wigto
Orkney, Argyllshire, Caithness, Roxbur
and in Lancashire.

These courses have been organised
Horticultural and Forestry Industry T
whom further details may be obtained.

Training Film

The Stewartry Drystane Dyking Com
pleted a Film Strip in colour, with acc⊙⊙
explain the building of a dyke. This is av

Dry Stone Walling Association

This was formed in 1968 by the Stewar
Committee and is open to Craftsmen Wall⊖
all interested in preserving the Craft in Gr·
anywhere.

Enquiries have *inter alia* been received
tralia, New Zealand, France, Germany, a
Great Britain.

A News Letter is sent out periodically
to keep everyone in touch.

Information

Miss Audland acts as Hon. Secretary o
Drystane Dyking Committee and the
Association and will with pleasure answ·
further information. Address: Cally Estat⊖
of-Fleet, Scotland, DG7 2HX.

4

Two Galloway dykers repairing a 4 foot 6 inch open dyke. The artist, Mason Trotter, RSA, has not shown the guiding strings. Isle of Man in the far distance.

The Author's two-year-old great-grandson Neil Rainsford-Hannay.

Dry Stone Walling

by

COLONEL F. RAINSFORD-HANNAY
c.m.g., d.s.o.

STEWARTRY OF KIRKCUDBRIGHT
DRYSTANE DYKING COMMITTEE

Gatehouse-of-Fleet

Kirkcudbrightshire

First published in mcmlvii
by Faber and Faber Limited
24 Russell Square London WC1
Second Edition published by the
Stewartry of Kirkcudbright Drystane
Dyking Committee in mcmlxxii
Printed in Great Britain by
Grieve the Printers Ltd
Dumfries

ACKNOWLEDGMENTS

I wish to acknowledge the great help given me over this book by Mr. Brian Vesey-Fitzgerald and also the encouragement by Mr. F. V. Morley, to whom I owe a great deal. The advice and experience of my two dyker friends, the late Mr. John Broadfoot of Sanquhar and Mr. John McKie, have been invaluable.

My thanks are also due to the following for photographs: For plates 2a, 2b, 3a, 3b, 4a, 13a and 13b to Mr. George J. Edwards of Newton Stewart; for plates 4b and 14a to Mr. J. Allan Cash of 82 Eton Hall, London E.C.3; for plates 5a, 5b and 6 to Mr. J. D. Rattar of Lerwick; for plates 7a and 7b to Mr. Alec Cain of Aberdeen; for plates 10b and 14b to Mr. David Innes of Currie; for plates 11a, 11b, 12a and 12b to Mr. Edwin C. Peckham of Stroud; for plate 15a to the Madeira Tourist Board and for plates 16a and 16b to Mr. Wilkes of Canada. The balance of the photographs, with the exception of plate 10a, were taken by the author.

Acknowledgments—Second Edition

The Stewartry Drystane Dyking Committee wish to express their gratitude to Mrs. Rainsford-Hannay and her family, to Mr. T. Farries of Blacklock Farries & Sons Ltd., Dumfries, for advice, to Messrs. Faber and Faber Ltd. for their help, and to Mr Douglas Low of *The Scottish Farmer* for the use gratis of the photographs of Neil Rainsford-Hannay.

CONTENTS

ILLUSTRATIONS

DIAGRAMS

Chapter I

PREHISTORY

The craft of dry walling, which means building in stone without mortar or cement, must be very old. How old we do not know.

When some genius of, perhaps, later Neolithic times discovered the virtues of mortar, the ancient builders must have jumped for joy, for it meant that they could use much less stone in their building. Their erections could be held together by mortar and not by the weight and accurate fitting of the stones which they used. They could rely on the binding quality of mortar and ignore some of the basic principles of dry stone building, principles that their forbears had developed. But it is interesting to note that their prehistoric erections built 'dry' have outlasted later erections where mortar was used.

Roman and Greek temples, and temples of much older date, are standing yet, but they do not owe their survival to the quality of mortar used in their construction, for of course mortar was used. No, these survivals owe their continued existence to the accurate fitting and setting of large dressed stones. The mortar has long since been fretted out by the wind and the rain of the centuries.

It would take a lifetime of research to examine the Palaeolithic and Neolithic structures of the Stone Age in an attempt to discover when mortar was first employed.

The Old Testament takes us far back, but nothing like far enough. The prophet Ezekiel says in Chapter xiii, verses 10 and 11:

> 'And one built a wall and daubed it with untempered mortar.

Say unto them that daubed it with untempered mortar, "Lo! it shall fall".'

And again in Chapter xxii, verse 28:

'Her prophets have daubed them with untempered mortar.'

The prehistoric dry stone builders could only put a roof, in the shape of a set of long stones, on very narrow chambers. Before the days of mortar they confined their skill to erecting mausoleums and open air temples.

No wonder it was called the Stone Age for stone was just all the material available to prehistoric man; stones and the skins of wild animals and possibly withies for baskets. The first real tool was a piece of stone with some kind of chipped out edge fastened to a stick with thongs.

Stones were big and heavy and so men worked in gangs, under task masters and under close supervision. The individual man who might fancy doing something for himself in the matter of a house, just had to make shift with what he could find—and lift. If he was lucky he might find a good dry cave; if not he might achieve a wattle and daub hut.

There are two peculiar specifications in the Old Testament:

I Kings vi, verse 7. The temple was built of 'stone made ready before it was brought hither, so that there was no hammer, nor axe, nor any tool of iron heard in the house while it was in building.'

This must mean that quarry dressed stones, accurately cut and probably numbered, were used.

And in Exodus XX, verse 25, we find:

'And if thou wilt build me an altar of stone, thou shalt not build it of hewn stone, for if thou lift up thy tool upon it, thou hast polluted it.'

This can only mean that they used random stones straight off

more tools and follow the same simple rules
followed many centuries ago.
oday?

the gr
of mor

There
enactmen
sense. For
and litter o
with gentle c
would burn m

We can go ba
Egypt, to about
construction but
In the later dynast
material being ofter
always good.

So even 4700 B.C. c
mortar. There seems to
though it is. It must of c
One can only conjecture
discover mortar. Perhaps it
dig for lime or gypsum depc
Bronze and Iron Ages.

The designers of the Tower
burnt bricks and 'slime'—whate
the time of Alexander the Great a
and archaeologists think that morta
of the ancient city of Jericho, a tent
rather earlier than the earliest pyram

So perhaps we may place the earlies
than 5000 B.C. and later than the end
all parts of the world.

An unsatisfying and vague solution. Bu
craft of dry stone work goes back to the ea
that where stone is plentiful it has persisted
present day.

It is one of the very very few crafts quite
unspoilt by modernity. Dry stone craftsmen-

craftsmen—use no
that their forbear
Now what of t

13

the ground in the best dry stone tradition. There is no mention of mortar; perhaps it would have also 'polluted it'.

There will have been ritualistic reasons for both these enactments, but behind ritual there is often plain common sense. For the temple, the intention was not to have a vast mess and litter of stone chippings. For the altar, the sacrificial fire, with gentle currents of air rising through the dry stone work, would burn much better than on a cemented slab of stone.

We can go back much further still; to the earliest pyramids of Egypt, to about 4700 B.C. Mortar was certainly used in their construction but the huge stones were most accurately fitted. In the later dynasties the interior work was more sketchy, the material being often mud bricks, but the outer masonry was always good.

So even 4700 B.C. does not take us back to the discovery of mortar. There seems to be no record of that date, important though it is. It must of course have varied all over the world. One can only conjecture why men of the Stone Age did not discover mortar. Perhaps it was that they had not the tools to dig for lime or gypsum deposits. Those tools came later in the Bronze and Iron Ages.

The designers of the Tower of Babel intended to build with burnt bricks and 'slime'—whatever that may be. The Greeks of the time of Alexander the Great are known to have used mortar and archaeologists think that mortar shows in the lower courses of the ancient city of Jericho, a tentative date being 5000 B.C. rather earlier than the earliest pyramid.

So perhaps we may place the earliest use of mortar as earlier than 5000 B.C. and later than the end of the Neolithic Age in all parts of the world.

An unsatisfying and vague solution. But we can say that the craft of dry stone work goes back to the early age of man, and that where stone is plentiful it has persisted as a craft until the present day.

It is one of the very very few crafts quite unaffected and unspoilt by modernity. Dry stone craftsmen—and they are craftsmen—use no more tools and follow the same simple rules that their forbears followed many centuries ago.

Now what of today?

Chapter II

STONE WALLING SINCE THE
SEVENTEENTH CENTURY

Dry stone walls, dry stane dykes! How does the ordinary reader, the man in the street, the holiday maker, the countryman, regard these objects which meet him everywhere in the west and north-west of these islands? In the phraseology of today, what are his reactions? Does he—or she—look upon them with any sort of interest or do they just merge into the landscape as part of the infinite variety of hills, rivers, lakes, fields, woods and farms?

Some people do look upon these walls with interest and even with wonder, but many more do not. The vast majority, though, in the course of their lives they see thousands—yes, thousands—of miles of such walls, take them as a matter of course and seldom give them even a passing thought.

Yet here we have a native art, unsurpassed elsewhere. In other lands of the eastern hemisphere there are, of course, such walls, many thousands of miles of them, but they are rarely up to the standard that British dry stone wallers can show. It is an art that has persisted through the centuries and that now—even in this age of steel—more than holds its own.

But many people are interested and their number is growing. For in these days of motoring, expensive though it is, we do get about our land far more easily than ever did our great-grand-parents. Their view of the rural scene was limited to what might catch the eye when seated in a railway carriage.

From a train the observant traveller can get a general view of the state of crops, the abundance, or otherwise, of the harvest, the progress of cultivation and the varying types of soil. But

15

from a train the most keen-eyed and knowledgeable traveller will get but a fleeting glimpse of any work going on. For more than half the time, the train runs through industrial areas or through cuttings. Even though he may have a window-seat and the day be clear, the traveller by train seldom sees a craftsman at work, seldom sees a hedger pleaching a hedge, or a forester felling a tree. I have never yet seen a pack of hounds from the train, although I often ride an imaginary line after a ghostly pack, on the perfect horse of fantasy, as my train speeds through the Shires.

From a motor car far more of the countryman's activities can be seen, especially by the passengers. On a cycling or a walking tour one comes right up against them; and those who elect to take a riding expedition through the lanes and by-ways of the land, will find matters of interest for their inquiring minds in every hedge, every dry stone wall, every gate and every cottage.

And, speaking of the inquiring mind, here are some questions which are frequently asked about the miles of dry stone walls, where these form the usual type of fence.

The first question is nearly always: 'Where on earth did they get all those stones and how were they carried up those hills?'

The answer is easy. The stones were quarried close to the walls from outcrops of rock visible still. No dry stone-waller ever carries a stone uphill if he can possibly help it, he rolls or sleds it down to the job.

Another question would be: 'Why did they not use posts and rails, or posts and wire?'

Two hundred years ago there were few woods on the moors, so that all material, except stone, would have to be carried up-hill. There was no fencing wire in those days.

Another favourite question is: 'How could the dykers hoist those great stones so high on to the dyke?' With a two inch board, four or five feet long, and a working knowledge of lever-age, two wallers without straining themselves can deal with stones as big or bigger than a steamer trunk.

Stone walls without mortar are usually called dry stone walls,

2a. 4 ft. 9 ins. dyke built in 1778. A close-up view with a low double

2b. View of same dyke as above

and in Scotland, dry stane dykes. In the pages that follov
will hold to that nomenclature: dry stane dykes whe
Scotland—dry stone walls anywhere else. They have been
as fences from the earliest times. They are such common ob
of the rural upland scene that they attract little more than ca
attention. It is difficult to find any mention of them in e
European history, but undoubtedly they existed, if only
enclose a few small yards round the dwellings of primit
farmers.

In our own islands, in Brittany, Italy, Greece, Palesti
everywhere where stone was suitable, men with no mechani
aids, other than a wooden lever and an appropriate fulcru
shifted huge blocks of stone, to enclose fields, to fence roa
sides, often to make a grave.

One has only to observe the many stone circles from Cornwa
to Stonehenge and on to the Shetlands, all the Palaeolithic an
Neolithic remains, to realize the amount of clever craftsmanshi
employed by what we are sometimes pleased to call our wil
and woolly ancestors.

Photo 1b shows an interment site of 1500 B.C. It wa
excavated by an archaeological society in 1949. Up till this
date, there was a long grass-covered barrow with some upright
stones at one end of it. These stones then stood some four feet
above the ground. Excavation showed a small semicircular
court at the feet of these monoliths, which are now eight or
nine feet high.

Dykers of 200 years ago built a dyke across one end of the
barrow or long cairn—the photograph shows this—but they
did not use the tall stones of the interment site, so perhaps our
forefathers of two hundred years ago were not so iconoclastic as
they may seem to have been.

Romulus, assisted, or impeded, by his brother Remus, built
the early walls of Rome. Remus, we are told, was work-shy and
no dyking enthusiast. He was for ever taunting his industrious
brother and one day he went too far, jumping and pushing over
the walls as they rose steadily under the devoted hands of

Romulus. Perhaps at that early stage, Romulus had not learned about the binding qualities of the 'through band'. The demise of Remus, at the hands of his infuriated brother, would appear as an act of perfectly justifiable homicide to every earnest dry stane dyker. As a passing thought, one never hears of anyone named Remus, unless he is a plantation negro.

As stated before, Europe and Asia Minor have thousands of miles of such walls especially among the terraced lands of such wine-growing districts as Tuscany. But it is doubtful if any dry stone walls outside these islands can bear comparison with our British dykes. This, however, is a field for other pens than mine. The pages that follow are intended to show the value of the dry stone walls that enclose the fields of a very large part of these islands and of many parts of the Continent.

They fence in our stock with welcome shelter; their very making has cleared the ground of stones and made cultivation possible; and they enable our farmers and shepherds to get their land cropped and grazed with the regularity necessary to good farming.

It will be asked: 'Why write a book about this simple matter? Why tell the farmer what he should know all about? Why, in homely phrase, try to teach your grandmother how to suck eggs?'

The reader can very readily get an answer to these questions. Let him go to any farmer and ask him for the name of a skilled dry stone waller and how to get the man's services for some work in the country. Seated at his fireside, he can pick up the telephone and get an answer in a minute or two. The answer will most certainly be that such men are scarce. The fact is that in many districts the craft is dying out. If the farmer is asked if he can do the work himself, in four cases out of five the answer will be NO. He will say that he can pile up stones on top of each other to fill a gap, but will admit that he cannot make a permanent job of a much needed repair. He makes shift to fill a gap with anything that comes to hand.

An extreme, but not unusual case will be that of a man who

1a. Big stones high in the dyke

1b. Prehistoric burial site of Paleolithic era. Excavated on Cairnholy Farm in 1947

will spend quite a time catching a horse, yoking it to a cart and loading up with two or three old bedbacks and then going a mile to stuff this evidence of incompetence into the gap. He should have been able, in the time, to repair a stretch two yards wide with the stones on the spot, and well enough to last for another generation at least; indeed, for much longer if he were a skilled dyker himself.

This is certainly an extreme case, but it throws into relief all those farmers and owners who look to their dykes as a matter of routine. Some give them a few days' work in early summer, some by the better plan of insisting on repairing at once. This will mean little more than replacing any fallen coping stones and tightening up the cope here and there. But the former plan had best be entrusted to a professional dyker.

The many finely fenced farms that are a pleasure to see give very little trouble to their occupiers as long as a minute or two is spent on replacing the occasional fallen stone. This may not be necessary for weeks on end; long stretches will require no attention for years.

Chapter III

FENCES AND THE ENCLOSURE ACTS

There is a question which, as far as I know, has never been posed. A question implies an answer, and the person who might give the answer should have had a very particular background. I have not yet been able to find the right person to whom to pose this question.

The suitable person would be one whose entire life had been spent in what the emigration offices called the wide open spaces of Australia or South Africa, or on the prairies of North America, and who had had no other environment.

Having recruited such a person with the stated qualifications, and landed him safely at Southampton, let us conduct him to a comfortable seat by the window in an aeroplane and let us accompany him, on a fine clear day, on a flight northwards over the length of England and Scotland as far as the river Tay, flying via Romsey, Warwick, Buxton, Manchester, Skipton, Carlisle, Lanark and Stirling. Having taken a passage in the same aeroplane, we would tell him that, on our arrival at Perth, we would ask him what had struck him most about the scenery outside the towns.

In spite of, perhaps because of, his early environment, our friend is interested and articulate, so that he will assuredly say that he never could have imagined such a bewildering pattern of hedges, stone walls, roads, lanes and woods. A little prompting on our part would elicit from his wonder and admiration of the skill and industry which brought these fences into being.

How many of us know that this irregular patchwork of hedges and walls did not exist before 1760 north of the Thames, and that the work was fairly complete only by 1850?

It is true that the south-east of England, parts of Sussex and

Chapter III

FENCES AND THE ENCLOSURE ACTS

There is a question which, as far as I know, has never been posed. A question implies an answer, and the person who might give the answer should have had a very particular background. I have not yet been able to find the right person to whom to pose this question.

The suitable person would be one whose entire life had been spent in what the emigration offices called the wide open spaces of Australia or South Africa, or on the prairies of North America, and who had had no other environment.

Having recruited such a person with the stated qualifications, and landed him safely at Southampton, let us conduct him to a comfortable seat by the window in an aeroplane and let us accompany him, on a fine clear day, on a flight northwards over the length of England and Scotland as far as the river Tay, flying via Romsey, Warwick, Buxton, Manchester, Skipton, Carlisle, Lanark and Stirling. Having taken a passage in the same aeroplane, we would tell him that, on our arrival at Perth, we would ask him what had struck him most about the scenery outside the towns.

In spite of, perhaps because of, his early environment, our friend is interested and articulate, so that he will assuredly say that he never could have imagined such a bewildering pattern of hedges, stone walls, roads, lanes and woods. A little prompting on our part would elicit from his wonder and admiration of the skill and industry which brought these fences into being.

How many of us know that this irregular patchwork of hedges and walls did not exist before 1760 north of the Thames, and that the work was fairly complete only by 1850?

It is true that the south-east of England, parts of Sussex and

will spend quite a time catching a horse, yoking it to a cart and loading up with two or three old bedbacks and then going a mile to stuff this evidence of incompetence into the gap. He should have been able, in the time, to repair a stretch two yards wide with the stones on the spot, and well enough to last for another generation at least; indeed, for much longer if he were a skilled dyker himself.

This is certainly an extreme case, but it throws into relief all those farmers and owners who look to their dykes as a matter of routine. Some give them a few days' work in early summer, some by the better plan of insisting on repairing at once. This will mean little more than replacing any fallen coping stones and tightening up the cope here and there. But the former plan had best be entrusted to a professional dyker.

The many finely fenced farms that are a pleasure to see give very little trouble to their occupiers as long as a minute or two is spent on replacing the occasional fallen stone. This may not be necessary for weeks on end; long stretches will require no attention for years.

Romulus. Perhaps at that early stage, Romulus had not learned about the binding qualities of the 'through band'. The demise of Remus, at the hands of his infuriated brother, would appear as an act of perfectly justifiable homicide to every earnest dry stane dyker. As a passing thought, one never hears of anyone named Remus, unless he is a plantation negro.

As stated before, Europe and Asia Minor have thousands of miles of such walls especially among the terraced lands of such wine-growing districts as Tuscany. But it is doubtful if any dry stone walls outside these islands can bear comparison with our British dykes. This, however, is a field for other pens than mine. The pages that follow are intended to show the value of the dry stone walls that enclose the fields of a very large part of these islands and of many parts of the Continent.

They fence in our stock with welcome shelter; their very making has cleared the ground of stones and made cultivation possible; and they enable our farmers and shepherds to get their land cropped and grazed with the regularity necessary to good farming.

It will be asked: 'Why write a book about this simple matter? Why tell the farmer what he should know all about? Why, in homely phrase, try to teach your grandmother how to suck eggs?'

The reader can very readily get an answer to these questions. Let him go to any farmer and ask him for the name of a skilled dry stone waller and how to get the man's services for some work in the country. Seated at his fireside, he can pick up the telephone and get an answer in a minute or two. The answer will most certainly be that such men are scarce. The fact is that in many districts the craft is dying out. If the farmer is asked if he can do the work himself, in four cases out of five the answer will be NO. He will say that he can pile up stones on top of each other to fill a gap, but will admit that he cannot make a permanent job of a much needed repair. He makes shift to fill a gap with anything that comes to hand.

An extreme, but not unusual case will be that of a man who

and in Scotland, dry stane dykes. In the pages that follow we will hold to that nomenclature: dry stane dykes when in Scotland—dry stone walls anywhere else. They have been used as fences from the earliest times. They are such common objects of the rural upland scene that they attract little more than casual attention. It is difficult to find any mention of them in early European history, but undoubtedly they existed, if only to enclose a few small yards round the dwellings of primitive farmers.

In our own islands, in Brittany, Italy, Greece, Palestine, everywhere where stone was suitable, men with no mechanical aids, other than a wooden lever and an appropriate fulcrum, shifted huge blocks of stone, to enclose fields, to fence road-sides, often to make a grave.

One has only to observe the many stone circles from Cornwall to Stonehenge and on to the Shetlands, all the Palaeolithic and Neolithic remains, to realize the amount of clever craftsmanship employed by what we are sometimes pleased to call our wild and woolly ancestors.

Photo 1b shows an interment site of 1500 B.C. It was excavated by an archaeological society in 1949. Up till this date, there was a long grass-covered barrow with some upright stones at one end of it. These stones then stood some four feet above the ground. Excavation showed a small semicircular court at the feet of these monoliths, which are now eight or nine feet high.

Dykers of 200 years ago built a dyke across one end of the barrow or long cairn—the photograph shows this—but they did not use the tall stones of the interment site, so perhaps our forefathers of two hundred years ago were not so iconoclastic as they may seem to have been.

Romulus, assisted, or impeded, by his brother Remus, built the early walls of Rome. Remus, we are told, was work-shy and no dyking enthusiast. He was for ever taunting his industrious brother and one day he went too far, jumping and pushing over the walls as they rose steadily under the devoted hands of

2a.   4 ft. 9 ins. dyke built in 1778. A close-up view with a low double

2b.   View of same dyke as above

1a. Big stones high in the dyke

1b. Prehistoric burial site of Paleolithic era. Excavated on Cairnholy Farm
in 1947

most of Wales had been enclosed long before, but most of England and Scotland was open country and one could ride from London to York, like Dick Turpin, without any impediment, taking to the open country when the toll-gates came in sight. Dick Turpin during his famous ride need not have jumped a fence.

There were, of course, fences close to villages and which constituted the 'infield', but the 'outfield' or 'waste' of each parish and manor was not fenced at all.

The outfield was common grazing, numbers of cattle and sheep being kept out during the summer and tended mostly by children. In winter the stock would be brought in, under what cover there was, and fed on what could be spared from the infield; but most of the animals would have to be slaughtered and salted down. One would not have thought that the disease of scurvy would have had anything to do with fences, but the wholesale slaughter of cattle and sheep at the end of the grazing season resulted in no fresh meat all through the winter months. Scurvy and other skin diseases affected even the households of the great. G. M. Trevelyan tells us that even the Russells and the Verneys were not exempt.

The Enclosure Acts, which did enable the land to be fully cultivated, met with fierce opposition from copyholders, peppercorn renters and similar small people and injustices were done to people who looked upon the waste or outfield as partly their own. Money compensation did not make up for the loss of this common grazing, scanty though it was. These smaller landholders had to change from a life of penury but independence which they liked, to one of regular wages, to which they objected violently. But the benefits which the resulting agriculture conferred on the soil and on the nation outweighed the seeming injustices to the many independent small landholders.

Later, when all children of school age had to go to school, enclosure of the land was approaching completion and fences took the place of those small shepherds and shepherdesses. There was a period of between twenty and forty years, however, before the Education Acts came fully into force, when the children still watched the grazing in the fenced fields. It has been said that the fields were more evenly grazed when children looked after the grazing. In Scotland they did their schooling in the winter.

Now a white-tiled, air-conditioned set of school-rooms claims them. Seldom during spring do we see country children taking a real part in the working of the countryside except, perhaps, at the potato harvest and at odd times during the hay and corn harvest. All through the joyful weeks of spring and early summer, when the rural scene is at its best, the children are at their desks, each qualifying for the post of a cog in a cumbersome nationalized machine. Their great-grandparents tended the flocks, generally in pairs. They were out all day throughout the months of spring, summer and early autumn. They benefited greatly in health and in mind, for nature blossomed and burgeoned all round them. They learnt the signs of the weather, the names of the trees and flowers and the ways of wild life. One has only to look up the many names that every tree and wild flower has been given to realize how this country lore originated.

The children knew how and where to take shelter and little that happened in the countryside escaped them. But sometimes their attention wandered and so we get two lovely little nursery songs: 'Little boy blue, come blow your horn—the sheep is in the meadow, the cow's in the corn'. Once aroused, little Boy Blue would quickly clear cow and sheep out of these carefully tended preserves of winter fodder. He probably 'got away with it', but not so Little Bo-Peep.

'Little Bo-Peep she lost her sheep—and doesn't know where to find them.' That was a much more serious matter, for her father would have to go out to find and gather them, and make peace with his neighbours. Poor wee woe-begone lassie! but someone comforted her, perhaps her small partner who was as much to blame as she was.

'Let them alone and they'll come home,

And bring their tails behind them.'

Was it Bo-Peep who gave those charming names to the hanging fruit of the alders and willows?

One would wish to expand this line of thought—some might call it fantasy—and it does seem a pity to have to come back to our stony subject with a bump, but we may do so with the conviction that these little songs could never have been composed after the passing of the Enclosure Acts.

Dry stane dyking, in a comprehensive way, was first undertaken on the lands of Palgown in the west of the Stewartry of Kirkcudbright. Somewhere about 1710, when the early Enclosure Acts were passed, the brothers McKie (the reputed descendants of the old woman who gave shelter to Robert the Bruce in the wilds of Galloway and gave him also her three sons as henchman) leased pieces of land free to people who would work for them in the summer.

In the spring, these people took to the hills with tents of sorts, and poles. In a very few days they had built themselves huts of turf and stone. Heather thatched the roofs and heather made their beds. The huts can have differed very little from the shielings to which Highlanders migrated every year on the first of May, for the summer grazing. The brother McKie were their own foremen, and in a year or two many square miles of otherwise useless land were enclosed by dry stane dykes, fine strong erections, and the value of the McKie's lands was increased at least fourfold.

This example was quickly followed. Right through the eighteenth century and well into the nineteenth, thousands of miles of dykes were built all over Scotland and in many parts of England.

The best and tallest dykes, running up to six feet, are the march dykes between Estates. The later work after 1840, with so much experience behind it, seems to be the best, but the photograph No. 2 of the dyke built in 1778 shows fine craftsmanship.

In some districts the passing of the Enclosure Act did not

affect the smaller farmers and freeholders. For instance, in the dales of the Lake District these 'statesmen' had for many years fenced their land with stone walls and for generations stones off their small fields had added to their height and been used to build new walls. It is true, as Wordsworth the poet has said, that the numbers of these statesmen had been halved, and the size of their holdings doubled by amalgamation, but the walls remained and are there now for all who care to see. This lessening in numbers and increase in acreage was directly due to the invention of the spinning jenny, which concentrated spinning in factories and deprived the dale women and their children of profitable work. Therefore, the holdings had to be doubled to support these families.

Again, in Wales, while there are some large estates, the actual farms are small in extent, and are fenced with stone walls and turf banks erected generations before the Enclosure Acts. Stone was the best material available. Some of these Welsh walls must be very old indeed.

The same conditions apply to Northumberland, where the land had been enclosed for many years and only two per cent of it came under the Enclosure Acts. Nor was Cornwall or the south-west of England much affected. It was already enclosed, as was the whole of Kent, parts of Essex and east Sussex. The reasons, which vary in every case, for these early enclosures, need not be entered into here.

Chapter IV

MERITS OF DRY WALLING

The word dyke has, of course, two meanings. In Romney Marsh and in East Anglia it means a deep V-shaped ditch, steep sided with a bank often on one or both sides: in Scotland it means a wall built of stones without mortar.

There is no similarity between a wet earth ditch in Lincolnshire and a dry stone wall in Galloway, but they are both excellent fences and neither owe anything to imported material.

Dry stone dykers, busy at their work, and even when only moderately skilled, get much satisfaction with every movement they make. They are dealing with a separate problem with every stone they handle. If we look at a dry stone wall, we can see that countless little problems had to be solved with every stone. In this way the craft is a long way ahead of any other practised out of doors. Stand and watch a skilled man building such a wall. Aimlessly, it would seem, he picks up a stone for the double dyke, but with no hesitation he finds a place for it, a place where it breaks joint, where it finds a firm bed and where it supports its neighbours.

Unfortunately the interested visitor does not often get the chance of seeing work in progress. But he can often see a recent repair of a gap and by using a little thought can realize what clever conscientious work has been accomplished.

MERITS OF DRY STONE WALLS

1. They are durable. Many have stood for 200 years and look like standing for another century.

25

2. They are stock-proof against all stock except blackfaced sheep. If 5 feet 3 inches high, they are stock-proof against these.
3. They occupy very little ground, 34 inches at the base at most.
4. They give shelter at all seasons.
5. They can stand on ground where no post can be driven and where no hedge can grow.
6. They are cheaply maintained.
7. They drain themselves.
8. They can be surmounted by any careful person, without damage to the dyke or to the clothes of the climber.
9. They require no imported material.
10. They require few tools; a 4-pound hammer, a rough frame, a good piece of string and a foot rule meet all requirements.
11. They cannot be burnt.

DRAWBACKS

They have a few drawbacks:
1. They take time to build. One man can build little more than six yards of four and a half foot dyke in a day. In limestone districts, such as the Cotswolds and the High Peak of Derbyshire, seven yards a day is the average.
2. Clumsy climbing will dislodge top-stones. The remedy is to put in a stile or a wicket where people are wont to cross.
3. Trees swing in the wind and their roots will weaken the dyke. These trees are generally ash or sycamore trees, self sown. The remedy is obvious.
   These last two drawbacks are common to other forms of fence.
4. Inquisitive and bored horses out at grass, especially at gateways, are apt to nose off top-stones. A bit of barbed wire, judiciously placed, is a preventative.
5. Where a dyke borders a road on an embankment, small boys find it great fun to roll off the top-stones from the cope

down the slope. Various remedies suggest themselves, starting with the small boy himself.

For years, for more than half a century, and until about 1935, there has been a casual indifference to the dry stone walls of our land. When people are so minded, the very walls that protect the land meet with inexcusable ill-treatment not only from the public, but even sometimes from the occupiers of the land. Occasionally one sees a splendid dry stone wall, built by craftsmen 100 years ago, pulled down to let through a snorting juggernaut of a threshing machine and the gap remains an eyesore and a nuisance for weeks, until a skilled dyker can come and repair. A little forethought in placing the stacks would have avoided all this. A motorist changing a tyre will take a cope stone off a wall to hold a wheel and leave it lying. He cannot put it back as it was, but he might have tried.

Things have been better, it is admitted, during the last fourteen years—since dyking competitions began—but only about one estate agent in four knows the first thing about the construction, and as for agents who run estates from a town office, the matter is a closed book to them.

It can therefore be appreciated why organizations such as the National Farmers Union, with the shining exception of the Kirkcudbrightshire branch, pay no attention, nor do they give any advice. Another notable exception is the Royal Highland and Agricultural Society. But Farming Colleges ignore such down-to-earth activities as the upkeep of dry stone walls. As to the farming papers, they don't know and are wise, perhaps, to maintain a discreet silence. For when they have to reply to an inquiry, they get the answer wrong. Then, moving up to the highest levels, what an opportunity for the Minister of Agriculture! At no cost at all he can point to the value of well-maintained dry stone walls. In fact, by the export of wire to countries that have no hereditary race of hedgers and dry stone wallers, there should be many thousand pounds more of exports to benefit the Exchequer.

All honour, then, to those men and to those landowners who

through years of neglect have maintained the high standards that still exist.

Chapter V

NATURE'S MATERIALS

For centuries men have protected their land by means of fences made of local materials—nature's materials. In these islands, after the Enclosure Acts, fences of all kinds multiplied greatly. Where timber is plentiful, farmers use posts and rails, on fen lands deep ditches are the rule, and on the good soil of the lower country, thousands of miles of hedges have been planted and fostered, hedges mostly of whitethorn or quickset, the word 'quick' here meaning 'alive'.

In hilly districts, where stone outcrops abound, our forefathers concentrated on erecting dry stone walls, adapting themselves to the stone of the locality. Practice enabled them to handle quite shapeless masses of stone with consummate ease to assemble into strong durable and effective fences for their fields. It is only during the last sixty years that manufactured fencing material, including wire in its several forms, has come into use.

Natural fences do not advertise, any more than did the sturdy men who made them, but the advertisement pages of our agricultural papers give plenty of space to the artificial varieties —thereby adding to their cost.

Wire-netting against rabbits in fields and plantations is certainly wanted; it is also wanted for folding sheep on roots and clover if wattle hurdles cannot be got. But other wire might well be sold to countries that have no race of hereditary hedgers and dry stone wallers, to the great advantage of the Exchequer. An important point well worth the emphasizing.

In our moments of disappointment and disillusion and, in these later years of frustration, we feel helpless to arrest the process of decay, we view with dismay the gradual wearing out

29

of our buildings and of our worldly gear and plenishing. Pots and pans leak, clothes wear out, carpets become threadbare, curtains fade. Our very houses, spick and span though they may appear, imperceptibly harbour within their structure the seeds of decay. By no means behindhand are our own earthly bodies.

In this man-made world outside our doors we notice the same determined march of decay; roads are washed away, ditches fall in, carts ploughs, machines of all kinds rust away, and our wire fences quickly lose their early trimness.

True it is that timely repairs and coats of paint slow up nature's stealthy activities inside the materials of everything man has made for himself, but decay does go on.

It is a slow business, as a rule, this decay. But if fate decides that it should work more speedily it has an almost enthusiastic ally in Man himself. When Man is not crashing thousands of pounds' worth of aeroplane, or urging his motor car through roadside fences, or into some one else's vehicle, or into a town council's lamp standard, or over a county council bridge, he is in his own house, breaking glass and crockery, banging the hinges off the doors, smashing windows and providing a steady flow of rubbish for that unlovely heap of litter that he may, or may not, be able to hide.

But mark this: it is only Man's own handiwork that is so fated. Nature works very differently and if it were not for the never failing annual miracle of Spring, the countryman's outlook would be dismal indeed.

It may well be asked, what on earth has this to do with dry stone walls?

The point, it is hoped, has been made that everything manufactured by man is subject to decay. Now, this does not apply to our natural fences. Thorn hedges improve every year when properly looked after. Growth may be too exuberant and may have to be curbed, guided and controlled. But there is no decay that is not revived by vigorous young shoots.

Let us now consider our dry stone walls. There is nothing

manufactured about them, they are made from Nature's own crude materials and erected after a system that shows signs of an ancient genius. When so built, they will stand stiff and strong for centuries with a modicum of skilled attention, long after the dyker's own house has fallen into decay.

Why is this? And why is all our acquired skill in building, with the help of mortar and cement, made to look silly when compared with a well built dry stane dyke such as is shown in photograph No. 2? That dyke was built in 1778 and looks like lasting for as long again. It stands in Kirkcudbrightshire.

The answer is water: just that, water. Rainwater, helped by wind, in time gets through the best of masonry, and all sorts of things happen behind the coats of rough cast that cover our modern brickwork. Not so with our hedges and dry stone walls. Rainwater revives our hedges. Rainwater runs through our dry stone walls and affects them hardly at all in a century. And yet, we spend money on artificial fences that have no enduring quality, importing them from distant factories, and allowing the inherited craftsmanship of our hedgers and dykers to be forgotten.

Before entering any more fully into our subject, perhaps a digression may be forgiven. Let us climb to the top of any nearby hill and take a good look at the green and golden fields spread out below. The prospect is sure to be a fair one, with its patchwork of pasture, crops and woodland, with a village here and there nestling round its age-old church. It is not unduly marred by the smoke of a distant factory.

From our high ground we can see many square miles of land, criss-crossed with fences of all kinds. A simple calculation shows that with fields averaging ten acres, there are eighteen miles of fence to one square mile. This figure is probably an under-estimate, because no account has been taken of the double fences along roads and lanes, and of the smaller irregular en-closures. If we take the county guide-book of our own particular county and look up the number of square miles in it, and then multiply that figure by eighteen, the resulting total is astonishing.

31

In Kent and the West, and in Wales, enclosures are, as has been shown, of a much older date than in the Midlands and in the North, but in general these many miles of hedges and walls were made by our forefathers from the time the Enclosure Acts first became law. Thousands of men were employed in their making, millions of thorn quicks were raised in estate and other nurseries, millions of cubic yards of soil were dug for the ditches, thousands of miles of morticed oak posts and cleft oak rails supplemented the hedges, and millions of tons of stones were rolled and sledded off the land to make dry stone walls. No factory-made material was used—none.

We are heirs of all the ages, and in no sense is this saying more apt than in the matter of our natural fences. They are well worth our attention and the more we care for them, the less trouble will we suffer from our wayward animals. We must not just take our fences as a matter of course and look upon them with disfavour when, through our own neglect, they fail to keep in our stock. Now is our opportunity to turn all metal fencing over to export and to use, for ourselves, nothing but nature's own materials.

All over Scotland, the north of England, Wales, Cornwall, the Cotswolds and the limestone ridge running from south-west to north-east through Derbyshire, there are many thousands of miles of dry stone walls. There are seven thousand miles in Kirkcudbrightshire alone. The matter of material 'arranges itself', as the French say. On soil too thin to grow a hedge, stone lies close to the surface and can be quarried from nearby. On deep soil with no stones we grow hedges. And in some cases we meet a combination of dry stone wall and hedge.

The hedges are there waiting to be trimmed, or if overgrown, to be expertly pleached. The ditches can be cleaned to the benefit of the field drains, and the fallen coping stones of the dry stone walls are lying to hand, to be firmed up into those same walls and, with a little expert attention, to stand stiff and strong for a century or more.

3*a*.　March dyke 6 ft. 3 ins high with two sets of staggered throughbands.
Built in 1778 and never requires repair

3*b*.　A Galloway hedge, made in 1800. The best fence of all

set to connect with the side stones. Nothing but good hard stones should be used.

THROUGHBANDS: Long flattish stones—or at any rate stones with one flat side—a few inches longer than the width of the dyke. These are set at 36 inches centres or less. Their weight and their roughness help to 'tie' the stones of the double. Outside Scotland they are called 'throughs'.

COVERBAND OR COVERS: These also are throughbands. They are shorter than the main throughbands and are laid touching each other along the top of the double dyke.

CLONKS: Large stones in the single and below the cope.

COPE: Generally speaking, well-shaped stones packed and blocked tightly on the coverband of the double dyke.

LOCKED TOP: Where the cope consists of longish flat stones set vertically to form a level top.

FRAME: A plain wooden affair made to the section in the specification, as high as the top of the double dyke. It looks like the legs of a trestle. Four slats of wood and a cross-brace are all that is necessary.

BATTER: A dry stane dyke slopes backwards with a 'batter' on each side. A 6 foot dyke can be 34 inches wide at the grass and 14 inches wide at the top.

ROOD: A measure of length: 6 yards in granite districts, 7 yards in limestone districts. It is generally a day's work for one man.

LUNKY HOLE: A small rectangular opening sometimes made at the bottom of the dyke, to let water through and as a passage for sheep.

PINS: Small wedging stones, tapped into the interstices. They render the dyke rabbit-proof and give it a little more strength. As far as possible, and as far as the stones allow, pins should be brought up with the dyke during the building.

These words are those used in Galloway. Other districts have different words. 'Clonk' is a good expressive word but it cannot be found in a Scottish dictionary.

Naturally, specifications will vary according to requirements; the height, the stones, the site and the notions of the man paying for the work.

Here is the specification of the two dykes bordering the road leading from Gatehouse of Fleet to its railway station on the moors. They seem to have been built at the expense of the old Glasgow and South-Western Railway in 1865. The permanent way inspector or superintendent was the man named to approve of the work.

SPECIFICATION OF 4 FOOT 6 INCH DYKE

Height to be 4 feet 6 inches.

Foundation to be 32 inches wide and the base 26 inches wide at the lift or immediately above the foundation stones.

From there build to taper gradually to 14 inches wide at the top of the Double which is to be 3 feet 6 inches above the grass.

The Double to have both sides brought up together, having the stones properly blocked, laid close together, well hearted and packed in the centre, every stone doing its duty by its neighbour. The outer stones to lie with their ends generally inward, so as to stretch into the dyke as far as possible, for the better binding of the work. Water-worn stones are not to be used.

The Double to have one set of throughbands 21 inches above the grass as 1 yard centres, projecting slightly on each side.

The cover band stones on top of the double to project 2 inches on either side. From there each stone of the single to diminish gradually in width to the top, no stones to be less than 10 inches high and all well locked together.

An interesting point in this specification is the matter of water-worn stones. Much of this dyke—which is standing today—consists of rounded granite boulders. The rough pimply surface of these stones is a great help in building, for they grip well and do not easily slip past each other. Water-worn granite, on the other hand, can be as smooth as marble.

35

An omission is a condition about building up-hill. It is well known that all work should go uphill, but this should have figured as an item in the specification.

Taking this particular specification as it stands, the reader should study the coloured frontispiece and Diagram 1.

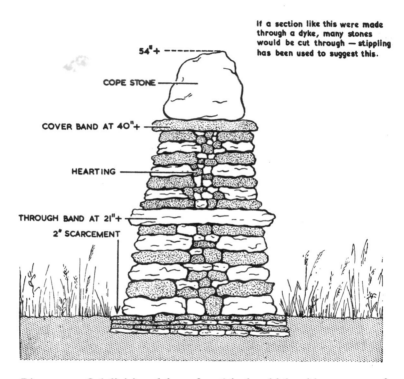

If a section like this were made through a dyke, many stones would be cut through — stippling has been used to suggest this.

54"+

COPE STONE

COVER BAND AT 40"+

HEARTING

THROUGH BAND AT 21"+

2" SCARCEMENT

Diagram 1. Subdivision dyke 4 feet 6 inches high with one row of throughbands at 21 inches above the grass.

The coloured frontispiece was painted by the late A. Mason Trotter, R.S.A. He took the opportunity of two men working opposite his house and between the three of them they brought out the fine points of double dyking. An omission is the guiding strings; the artist left these out.

Any other artist might have given an impressionist picture with no detail at all, but Mason Trotter had been repairing a bit of the wall himself and his foreground shows his own interest.

The line of the dyke to be built is carefully marked out by pegs. No doubt, two hundred or more years ago, when erecting march dykes, landowners came to give-and-take arrangements, whereby the dyke would avoid soft ground and run where suitable stone was accessible. Naturally, dykes are not built where there is no suitable stone. Where it is plentiful, it is quarried from higher ground and carted to its destination. A strong sled answers well on the hill. Often one sees a dyke running up a hollow, with all the marks of quarrying on the steep side slopes.

The necessary stones are laid out all along the site, if possible on both sides. The dyker does not want to move more than a yard from the job to pick up his material. Most stone is suitable —granite, basalt, whinstone, the harder limestones—but easily broken friable stone should not be used. When the land in Clydesdale was being enclosed two hundred years ago, stones were carted to the site in autumn, to lie weathering during winter, after which the hard suitable material could easily be picked out.

The foundation trench would be dug out to the firm subsoil: six inches is generally deep enough. This shallow trench is packed tight with hard flat stones, averaging the size of one's hand. If, however, a boulder happens to lie in the line of the dyke it should be incorporated with it. But the boulder must not provide a step for an active animal. The width of the trench is at least 4 inches wider than the base of the dyke. Strings are stretched accurately and tightly along either side of the trench to mark its course. After the foundation is ready, these strings are brought inwards 2 inches on either side and tied to the bottom of two frames, which are propped up vertically astride the trench. These frames are just a cross-section of the double dyke.

A double row of stones is then laid with their longer ends

37

stretching into the dyke and their outside faces touching the strings. The space inside is packed tight with good hard stones, the principle of 'breaking joint' being followed as far as possible and as the stones allow. Every hearting stone should be laid so as to help its neighbour by its rough surface and its shape.

For repair of gaps professional dykers seldom use frames; their eye is trained to keep the work in alignment. But they always build carefully to strings stretched between the sound portion of the dyke.

When the stones are fairly flat, as in limestone districts and in the Cotswolds, a very slightly outward and downward tilt is sometimes given to stones in the building of the double. This tilting helps to throw off the rainwater. This is, however, not done in Cornwall, where the stones are often tilted inwards and what rainwater there is runs through the centre of the work. With the much rougher stones of the North and in Scotland tilting can seldom be done.

As the work rises, the guiding strings are moved up the frames, At 21 inches above the grass, the throughbands are carefully laid, at not more than 36 inches centres. When there are plenty of such stones the intervals can be less. These throughbands should be fairly flat on the lower side and have a good bed on the stones beneath.

Dykes can often be seen with throughbands projecting as much as 8 inches on either side, just to show that they are throughbands. Cattle then will rub themselves against these projections. 1½ inches of projection is ample enough to ensure pressure on the outer edges of the double dyke. Some of the dykes in the High Peak district of Derbyshire show far too much projection of their 'throughs'.

After the throughbands are laid the dyke rises to about 42 inches above the grass and the dyke has narrowed to 14 inches wide. Here the cover band stones are laid on. These also are throughbands, shorter than those in the lower row, and should touch each other all along.

Now comes the point where the skilled man excels: the

locking of the cope stones. Previously he has laid these stones aside. For this particular dyke they should be 12 inches high and, very roughly, 12 inches across. He puts one at each end of his day's task and stretches a string tightly across their tops. Working from one end, and if on the slightest slope from the lower end, the skill is shown by the way every cope stone is firmly bedded and made to touch the top string and to fit into the irregularities of its neighbours. The rougher the stones, the tighter can they be made to sit. The cope can be tightened up still more by driving in a long thin wedging stone here and there.

Dykers like to start their work from an upright 'cheek' or scuntheon, that is a well-made pillar of well-shaped stones.

It is tempting to use long stones, with one smooth side, the wrong way in the double dyke, by laying them lengthwise on the outside to show a smooth surface, but a simple experiment will show how faulty this is. Take any stone that is a good deal longer than broad. Place this along the side edge of a table and close to the end edge. You can flick the thing sideways off the table with the little finger, but it would take much more force to pull or push it off endways.

Much skill is shown when building up hill, the stones being laid horizontally and not parallel to the slope. On a very 'stey brae' the dyker may have to build a succession of cheeks, with short pieces of double dyking between them. That, after all, is just what masons do.

A level, tight top is important as a deterrent to stock. An irregular bit at once attracts the attention of blackfaced sheep. I once watched a blackfaced ewe who detached herself from her friends and started on a deliberate tour of inspection of a dyke bounding a field in which she and a number of her kind were grazing. The dyke was four and a half feet high and a good one, but in two or three places near me the top looked a little loose. At each of these places, this adventuress stopped and stared. There was no expression whatever on that swarthy countenance. Twice she made a little run at the dyke, but baulked at the last moment. Finally, after a good walk round that field she

39

seemed to shake her silly head, shrug her woolly shoulders, then drifted sulkily back to her companions. The field into which she wanted to jump was a fresh field of young grass, but the dyke was just good enough to turn her.

I went to each of the places she had examined and in ten minutes had tightened up the cope to make the place safe for a long time to come. I did not inspect the rest of the dyke; the ewe had done that.

Some dykers used to pride themselves on being able to push a wheelbarrow along the top of their finished work, to show the importance of a level top.

A well-built dyke always looks well, but a badly hearted dyke can look well too. At all costs the temptation to show a good outside at the expense of a poor hearting must be avoided.

The Reverend Samuel Smith of Borgue, who compiled most of the survey of Galloway in the early eighteen hundreds, states: 'There is no operation connected with agriculture where so much depends on the honesty and integrity of the workmen'.

And John McTaggart in one verse of his 'Elegy to Davie the Dyker' epitomizes the whole matter:

> 'His dykes had ne'er the sleekit skin,
> All fair without and fause within;
> He did'na batter line and pin
> To please the 'ee.
> Ye niver heard a clankin din
> Whar biggit he.'

'Hearting' is a really good word. It means using every stone inside the double to support its neighbours, packing being tight and bedding surfaces made firm and level. 'Filling' is sometimes used, but hearting is the *mot juste*. Only good hard stones should be used, nothing small enough to get washed out by rain. It is fatally easy to take a shovel full of sand or soil here and there to level up the hearting and to make what looks like a good bed for bigger stones. But this means death to the dyke. The first winter's rain will wash out the smaller stuff and leave the centre hollow. The collapse in one or two places of a long stretch of excellent dyke is nearly always due to a careless workman employed at those places.

Outsiders, however interested they may be, can only see the outside and it is difficult for the most knowledgeable person to say what the inside is like, unless indeed he has watched the building. So a great deal must be left to the dyker's fidelity and pride in his craft. The many thousands of miles of excellent dykes still standing bear witness to much conscientious work.

A good dyker works fast. He likes, of course, well-shaped stones, but he prides himself on being able to deal with the roughest and most uncompromising material. He picks up a stone and down it goes into the one place made for it. Every facing stone is laid with its length stretching inwards. He breaks joint all the time. As far as possible he follows the principle that a vertical line through the centre of gravity of a stone should pass through the bedding surface. 'Pinning', when the dyke has been built, should be kept to the minimum. As far as the shape of the stones allows, it is best to get the pinning done while the building is going on, by preparing beds for the heavier stones. When pins are tapped in to fill in interstices, they must inevitably slightly alter the tight bedding of the bigger stones.

Chapter VII

COSTS

When a man ruefully contemplates a derelict dyke, derelict from his own neglect or from that of his predecessors, he may take comfort to his soul by reflecting that the material for repair is there, on the spot. The quarrying and the carting of the stones have been done and paid for generations ago. All he has to do in the way of preparation is to find a dyker, preferably two dykers, with their hammers and a few yards of string. And he will have the satisfaction of knowing that a reconditioned dyke is better than ever before, because the ground on which it stands has been consolidated by heavy pressure for a century or more.

But not being any more farseeing than most of us, he may find that he wants his fence made good in a hurry. He then considers the question of a post and wire fence, along the line of the derelict dyke. The objections to this undertaking are many. It gives no shelter, it lasts about eight years, a break at one point slackens the whole fence, the old stones lying about shorten the arable acreage on both sides and provide an unnecessary haunt for weeds and vermin. However, needs must for the ploughing programme is inexorable; so he puts up, we will say, a hundred yards of post and wire fencing.

What has he got? On the one hand he has an effective enough wire fence which will keep out lambs at the bottom, if it has been well erected. Its drawbacks have already been pointed out: one more may be added if the fence is on heather—the posts can be burnt.

On the other hand, if he decides on a dyke, it will take four times as long to build, but it will last for a century at least, and the farm will look as if it were well cared for.

But the wire fence may take longer than the farmer bargained for. He must order good posts, not so easily come by in these days, and also wire, and get these taken out to the job. A dyker, if available, can start work at once, for his material is all there spread out for him on the site.

Wages and costs are difficult to assess just now and perhaps the figures that follow are on the high side. They do show, however, the comparative costs in June 1952.

WIRE FENCE, 100 YARDS LONG

Six strands of wire, No. 8 gauge

60 larch posts 5½ feet at 1/9	£5	5	0
3 staying ,, at 4/–		12	0
2 end ,, at 6/–		12	0
630 yds. No. 8 wire for 6 strands	2	15	0
400 staples		2	0
Transport of posts and wire, say		10	0
2 men, 2 days at 15/– each	3	0	0
	£12	16	0

RECONDITIONING DRY STONE DYKE 4½ FEET HIGH

100 yards at 12 yards a day for two men
8 days, say 8½ days at £1 per man per day   17   0   0

Minor modifications may affect both these totals. For the wire fence ten per cent more posts may be needed to replace those which splinter when driven. The work may take longer, if the men have to use an iron crowbar on the presumably stony ground.

For the dyke, some extra stones may be asked for, but on the other hand the dyke from the grass up may not all require re-building.

These two totals are near enough together to engender food for thought. Let us hope that the man who pays the bill will look well ahead.

An old bill for dyking. These dykes, mostly 5 feet high, built 172 years ago are standing today. Long stretches that have not suffered abuse are stiff and stockproof as ever. They make an enduring testimonial to the fidelity of those old craftsmen John Cuningham and John McHarg. A rood of length equals 6 yards. Cost thus fivepence per yard at most.

Chapter VIII

VARIOUS FORMS OF DYKE

The dyke described earlier is the usual subdivision dyke. March dykes are much higher, from 5 feet 4 inches to 6 feet. These should have two courses of throughbands staggered, which means that the stones of the upper course are laid above the intervals of the lower one (diagram 3).

A third row of throughbands is often seen, especially in the High Peak district of Derbyshire. There is also a good example on the road between Penrith and Ullswater. It is 6 feet high on the road side, with two courses of staggered throughbands.

THE LOCKED TOP

A very tight form of coping was invented by John MacAdam of Craigengullich as far back as 1753. It is called the locked top.

This locked top coping consists of broad flat stones, nearly always of whinstone. The width of the top should be about 12 inches, not more than 2 inches thick, packed upright tightly together. The stones come out of whinstone beds and one can often see the quarried face in the neighbouring field. The dyker starts from one end and that the lower end. When the dyker has fixed a good length of this coping, he drives in specially chosen thin stones in several places. The result is a very firm top. This form is to be seen also in Ireland, but with thicker stones of varying height, to give the dyke a castellated appearance.

TWO WAYS OF USING UP BOULDERS

Many dykes are built with a high proportion of big stones. These can be used in two different ways. One method is shown

45

in Photos No. 2a and No. 2b. Here the double is quite low and the big stones are fitted above the double, as a single dyke. The big rough stones can be made to hold well together and are often fitted upright. Dykers can put up this form a good deal more quickly than the dyke just described in detail.

This kind of dyke is not very common, perhaps because a dislodged stone at the top unkeys a lot of others to make a wider and deeper gap. It can, however, be quickly repaired if repair is carried out at once.

A better way of using the big stones is by building what the Rev. Samuel Smith calls 'snecks'; another term is 'butt and hudd'.

Here short pieces of single dyke of the bigger stones are built, with stretches of double dyke between them. The effect is to tighten up the work and to divide it into panels. John MacAdam was also the inventor here. An observant fellow, indeed, who really studied how to use the varying shapes of stone to the best advantage for every separate dyke which he built.

GALLOWAY HEDGE

Another form is a combination of dyke and hedge. It was first invented by Hamilton of Baldoon in 1730, and copied extensively by Lord Selkirk of St. Mary's Isle. It is called a 'sunk fence' or a 'Galloway hedge'. It is perhaps best suited to ground when the dyke runs across a slope. It is often seen on roadsides where the ground falls towards the road. Our photograph No. 3b is a good example.

To make a sunk fence or Galloway hedge:

A right angled cut is made along the slope, the soil being thrown up hill. A double dyke is then built in the cut, one side being vertical against the upright cut. When the dyke reaches the height of the unstirred earth, long thorns are laid horizontally across the dyke with their roots in the soil above. The dyke is then raised to $4\frac{1}{2}$ feet and finished with a locked top. In two years the thorns turn up the face of the dyke and overtop it.

Many examples of this fence can be seen in the Gelston district and on the road between Castle Douglas and Creetown. There is a short stretch, the hedge being six feet high, in Academy Street, Castle Douglas. If it is intended to make one of these sunk fences, or Galloway hedges, the opportunity should be taken when both fields are in crop.

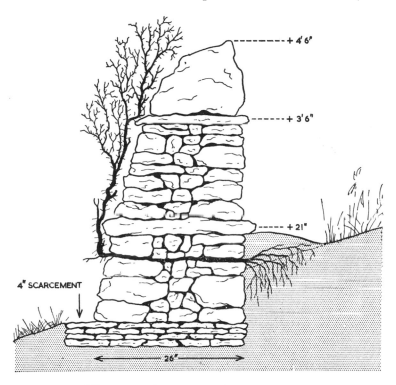

Diagram 2. Section of a Galloway hedge.

From the start a Galloway hedge is a formidable obstacle from one side, but on the other side, until the thorns are grown, it will not turn blackfaced sheep. After three years it defeats them. Practically no root cleaning is necessary, but the hedge as such requires a little attention every year. This last may be the reason why they are now not often made in a stonewall country.

47

These sunk fences, or Galloway hedges, when kept in order make really stock-proof obstacles. The functions of stone wall and thorn hedge are complementary to each other. The most vulnerable part of a dry stone wall is its cope, whereas the bottom of a hedge is most likely to become the weakest, so that the two together combine admirably.

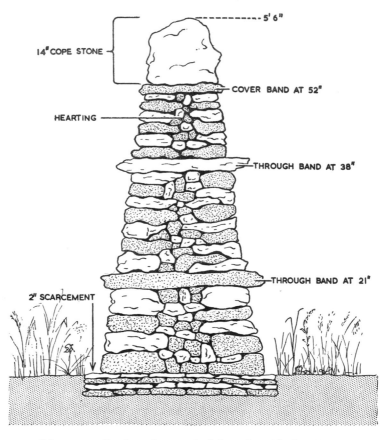

Diagram 3. Section of a march dyke 5 feet 6 inches high.
Double dyke up to 52 inches.
Second throughband though shown would be 'staggered'.

48

5a. Moussa Broch: on an uninhabited island of the Shetlands. Built against Danish pirates. All dry stone work, 2nd, 3rd and 4th centuries A.D.

5b. Clickiminn Broch: Lerwick, Shetlands. Built 2nd, 3rd and 4th centuries A.D. as shelter against Danish pirates

Chapter IX

THE GALLOWAY-DYKE

There is another form of dyke in Scotland which is sometimes met with, but the virtues of which have largely been forgotten. It deserves a chapter to itself. We hear of Galloway-Dykes, presumably because Galloway first specialized in dyking and the term is often loosely applied to any form of dry stone dyke.

But the authors from 1700 to 1724 of the *Survey of Agriculture in Scotland* write very definitely of a very special 'Galloway-dyke'. Those authors who compiled the survey of the counties of Argyll, Inverness, Stirling, Dumfries, Roxburgh, the Hebrides and Galloway, were sometimes parish ministers. No doubt, each one would delegate some of his task to fellow ministers whom he would meet regularly at presbytery meetings.

By these authors, the two words are written with a hyphen and sometimes with a small 'g', thus: *galloway-dyke*. This particular form of dyke was built in those counties especially against blackfaced sheep and, owing to one very special peculiarity, they state that sheep just refuse to jump it. What they say is supported by Sinclair's General Report (1814) and much later still by Professor Scott in his *Text book of Farm Engineering*, 1885.

This *galloway-dyke* is built to not less than 5 feet 3 inches high and 34 inches thick at the base. It is occasionally met with at 6 feet in height. It is built 'double' to about 40 inches above the grass, the usual hearting and throughbands being carried out. At 40 inches the cover bands are laid on, bringing the height to 42 inches.

Now comes the peculiarity. The next 22 inches and more consists of single dyke of big rough stones, laid and interlocking

50

and narrowing towards the top, but with wide interstices between them and the *light showing through*. No pinning is done in this portion. The light showing through seems to deter all stock including blackfaced sheep.

All these writers state unequivocally that cattle and sheep will not attempt such an obstacle, the light showing through makes it look too dangerous. Now this sounds odd and it is certainly not generally known. Dykers and many shepherds, when questioned, find it strange but I know of two gentlemen with extensive sheep farms who are convinced about the matter. In the High Peak of Derbyshire one or two very big flock masters have a similar sort of wall. They like it, because it lets through driven snow.

To avoid overloading the text, only one extract from the Inverness-shire report is given here; those of several other counties are given in the Appendix which should be studied.

The Inverness-shire Report says:

'These walls have such a tottering and alarming appearance that all kinds of stock are terrified to attempt them, and as an additional recommendation they require fewer stones and are more expeditiously built and last as long as double stone walls without lime.'

These bygone authorities vary somewhat over the building (see Appendix) but there is a most decided consensus of opinion about the way *galloway-dykes* 'deter and terrify sheep'. One occasionally sees a dyke on a skyline, the stones at the top making an almost lacelike pattern, especially with a westering sun behind them. Perhaps they do exhibit a tottering appearance.

It seems that many miles of galloway-dykes, to give them their earlier hyphen, were built but that the real point of the openwork top has largely been forgotten. Probably well meaning people went so far as to pin up the interstices, thereby frustrating the earlier intention. A Stirlingshire dyke, in the parish of Denny, seems to have been dealt with in this way by being pinned up.

And it may be because of this that the main reason for the galloway-dyke has been forgotten. A farmer dies, with his dykes in good order, but does not tell his son. A laird dies, with his son in India; a factor takes over after an interregnum, a shepherd changes but does not tell his successor. Yet the dykes must be there still. They require no attention because they do their job.

There are many crafts the knowledge of which has been lost for the want of foresight and records, such as the brewing of heather ale for one, and certain glazes for pottery for another.

We are not entitled to believe that, after the very considerable work done on these galloway-dykes in their lower courses, only a lazy man's top was put on to them. One has only to look at them critically to realize that a lot of skill went into the construction of the lower portion, the double, which is high enough to give shelter to sheep lying down. Then looking at the cope, we can see that the tight binding is completely absent and that a deliberate and successful attempt has been made to give the dyke a 'fragile and tottering appearance'. The photographs show this and they also show that the claim that they can be easily and quickly repaired is also true.

The dyke shown is the 'head dyke' on a hill farm on the slopes of Cairnharrow. The stretch is quite clearly divided into panels by large portions of single dyke. In between are pieces of double dyke to about $3\frac{1}{2}$ feet above the grass. All the top 24 inches or so consists of big rough stones fixed firmly with the light showing through. It is easy to see what good shelter this dyke affords to sheep and lambs from a north and north-east wind. The double dyke also reflects some of the heat of the sun. To a shepherd it must be a lovely sight to find his early lambs tucked up against the warmth of the 'double dyke' while a northerly wind whistles over and through the top of it.

The photographs have been taken from the low side where the ground has been cultivated. From the high or the moorland side, the light shows through very plainly, because the background from the level of a sheep is nearly always sky or sea. And it is the moorland side from which the sheep will want to jump.

From the low side the background is generally dark heather or bracken.

With the light background showing through the roughly poised stones in the top courses of a *Galloway dyke*, the deterrent to an adventurous ewe is highly effective. When studying such a dyke, one ought to stoop down to the height of a sheep. From that height, 18 inches above ground level, the dyke top looks most formidable; 'tottering and terrifying' as bygone writers would have described it.

The tourist travelling along Highland roads cannot expect to see these Galloway-dykes at near hand. Nearly always they run away up in the hills and are usually march dykes.

Chapter X

SHELTER

Every sentient being, when not occupied with labour or feeding, seeks some form of shelter during its hours of rest. When so occupied, human beings do not rest in the open—normally. When at work out of doors, they take their midday leisure in some form of shade or behind some form of windbreak.

Of course it is most pleasant on a balmy day to bask in the sunshine, and on a windy day to face the breeze and let the wind blow through your hair, but on reflection you do not do that for long, for somehow the pleasant and even rapturous sensation soon palls, and you seek a shadier spot or a place where the wind blows with less violence and where you can meditate and survey the landscape undisturbed.

When cattle are not grazing on a hot day in summer, they like shade although they are often to be seen either on high points where they can get away from flies or away out on the sands at low tide. Sheep, too, although they are to be found on wide shadeless lands, do make for shade at the hottest time of day. But it is the bitter wind that sends both these species to shelter, in hollows, behind hedges and stone walls where these exist.

A dry stone wall, 4½ feet high, is impervious to wind at three feet above the ground, and there is always shelter on one of the sides of a field.

During what Scottish shepherds call the 'bask' days of March and April, in fact during the lambing season, one often sees a row of early lambs tucked up against the southern and sunny side of a dry stane dyke. The sun may be shining but a bitter 'bask' wind will be whistling over the top of the dyke. The lambs are happy enough with a little of the sun's heat radiating off the dyke, while they await their next feed from their mothers busy cropping the herbage in the open. Surely a gratifying sight to any flockmaster.

At this difficult time of year when there is but little green growth, there is always a fresh bite to be found on the sheltered side of a dyke.

The 'black house' of the Western Highlands was designed in the first place as a shelter and with driving rain and battering winds without, it was always snug and warm. The best of them were built with two dry stane dykes with a filling of dry peat blocks between them. The inner wall would be 2 feet thick and the outer wall anything up to 4 feet thick at the base. The roof was always a difficulty owing to the lack of suitable material. Oat straw was used if good reeds could not be found.

The thatch would be brought low and inserted well into the peat, so that no wind could get under it. The whole building looked like a smooth rounded antheap and was well adopted to fend off the most furious blasts. There is a good example of the black house in the Highland Museum at Kingussie.

The influence of shelter may be felt up to twenty-four times the height of the shelter itself. Thus a dyke five feet high would give its last faint shelter at a distance of forty yards.

There has been a move lately to provide long belts of trees along the western shore of the Long Island of the Outer Hebrides as protection against the gales of the Atlantic. No doubt this would be effective and the wind would be tempered farther and farther on the protected side as the years go by and as the trees increase in height. But these belts of trees would have to be forty yards wide. The outer ten yards or so would be stunted, but they would divert the blast over themselves to the benefit of the remaining trees.

But suppose a long line of dry stane dyke were erected, fronting the Atlantic gales. It would not need to be continuous, but there would have to be a lot of it to cover all the exposed parts. Such a dyke would have more of a 'batter' on the exposed

55

than on the landward side. It would then throw the wind higher and farther than the calculated twenty-four times the height.

As proof of this statement one has only to watch, on a windy day, a high tide dashing against a sloping breakwater. The top part of a wave will just slop over the breakwater, but the high spray will be wafted many yards over the adjoining land. And those airborne particles of spray are a good deal heavier than the moving air.

Another point: a dry stane dyke can be put up on the stoniest land, and its very making will clear the land of some of its burden of stone. Trees can be planted behind the wall and will benefit by its shelter. The wall will give shelter from the day of its building, the belt of trees will take four years before any sheltering effect is apparent. The wall would not suffer from abuse by livestock, for there would be no animals between the wall and the sea. Thus favoured the wall should endure for centuries, outlasting many generations of men, and during its long life nurturing several generations of trees.

The wall should, of course, be built to a proper specification. Water-worn stone should not be used; if of necessity such stones are used, they must be split with the hammer and their smoothness removed. Any form of mortar or cement should be avoided like the plague. Careful siting of every stretch of wall is vital, preferably on ridges, to ensure the best protection to the fertile ground on the landward side.

From the Hebrides let us turn to another windswept land.

Twenty of the Shetland Islands are inhabited and their small crofts are fenced by dry stane dykes adequately enough maintained. But here we meet another form of shelter. All over the Shetlands are to be found the brochs. These were built as shelters against men and the men were the raiding pirates of the second, third and fourth centuries of our era. Some are in ruins, some are standing now stiff and immensely strong. The broch on the now uninhabited island of Moussa is 38 feet high and contains 10,000 tons of stone. The wall in this case was 20 feet thick to an inner passage 6 feet wide, and thence to an inner wall also about 6 feet thick.

The whole building is circular and encloses a yard about 40 feet in diameter. The entrance, only some 4 feet high, could be easily closed from the inside by boulders laid by for the purpose. In the thickness of the wall a stairway ran up to the ramparts at the top.

The first 25 feet would be built on a 'batter' or slightly sloping inwards, the next 13 feet of height would be vertical. All the building was in dry stone work and is a unique example of that craft.

These brochs are so numerous that we must conclude that they were vitally necessary. The building of one might have been a local extravagance, but when we find forty of them, their erection must have been a matter of sheer necessity.

The islanders would know that a piratical raid could only be a cut and run affair, perhaps between tides. Some warning could be expected and in three or four hours movable property (scanty enough), food, fodder and livestock would be rushed up by the islanders to the security of their broch. The raiders, disappointed at the empty houses, might then tackle the broch, but here what could they do?

A battering ram would have to be of the size of a ship's mast, for there are no trees on the islands. Treachery from the inside is all that is left. Any attempt at digging out stones at ground level would be fully exposed to attack from the top. The only alternative is undermining through solid rock—no amusement for pirates. Pickings off the islands would be scanty and far too dearly won. Fatter lands and richer booty were to be had farther south. Pirates have never been famed for hard and continuous labour.

The brochs were all built to a pattern and Mr. A. T. Cluness, who writes so informatively in his book about the Shetlands, says that they must have been built by some early Vauban who was able to command hundreds of men to collect thousands of tons of stone and to insist on the one specification. With him we can marvel at the concentration of purpose and determination of the islanders who must have been convinced of the value of their efforts. We can estimate the magnitude of the threat to their homes by the stupendous labour which these Picts undertook. The Suevi of the second century and the Danes of the third and fourth must indeed have inspired fear and loathing.

The Shetlanders have the brochs close to hand as the finest example of dry stone building. The parish church of Nesting was built entirely out of stones taken from a broch south of Harbister. The Broch of Easter, now a ruin, provided the stones for the laird of Melby to build a 6 foot high dry stane dyke 1,300 yards long and yet far less than half the stones were taken.

Brochs, and much dry stone work in old chapels and old kirkyards, are also to be found in the Orkneys. And, of course, the fences are all of dry stone work. There is nothing particular to be learnt here about the craft except in one island, that of North Ronaldshay. Here the island is carefully fenced internally but all round the seaward edge of the island is a high dry stane dyke 5 to 6 feet high. It keeps the sheep *off* the fertile land and *on* the shore. These little sheep live on the seaweed, and thrive on it. At the lambing the ewes are allowed on to special small grass fields for the sake of their milk supply, but at all other times seaweed is their food. The sheep are called keero sheep (Gaelic ciora), their wool is fine and soft and their meat tender, and the high perimeter dyke no doubt shelters part of the carefully cropped land.

Chapter XI

THE PROBLEM OF THE
BLACKFACED SHEEP

Blackfaced sheep, when badly herded, will learn to jump dykes. If our low ground heavy sheep, such as the Down breeds and the Leicester crosses, could live and thrive on heather our fencing problems would be simple. But we have the very active blackfaced sheep and because that breed is invaluable for crossing we must keep him, or rather her, within bounds. There are many ways of dealing with these creatures, although good shepherds who move their sheep morning and evening do not seem to have much trouble.

The most important dyke on a hill is called the 'head dyke'. It fences off the moorland and rough pasture from the arable ground. It should not be less than 5 feet 3 inches high on the moorland side and should be in good order with a level top. Usually it runs across a slope with a drop to the arable fields below. If, however, the dyke is under 5 feet 3 inches and the sheep have been carelessly herded, there is more than one way of stopping them.

One is to set a line of 7 feet long posts against the side of the dyke with two rows of wire stapled to the posts above the dyke. The posts, set 15 feet apart, can be light coppice poles creosoted, or light larch thinnings.

Another method is to fix 2 feet iron posts with lead into the dyke. These posts should be set 15 feet apart, and should support two lines of wire, the top wire being 18 inches above the cope. This is expensive and troublesome to erect, but answers well. These dykes can be seen along the railways in Lanarkshire and in Perthshire.

A third expedient (and perhaps the best and cheapest) is to use 3 foot posts, 3 inches in diameter, driven into the ground on the high side of the dyke. Four inches below the top of the posts a line of plain wire is stapled and stretched tight. Placed 18 inches from the dyke, this presents too great a jumping problem for our blackfaced friends. Two men can put up half a mile of this in a day, the posts being 15 feet apart. In every one of these cases the dyke should be first topped up level.

Let us hope that our blackfaced ewes will not learn to gallop at this last obstacle and take off like Royal Tan over Beecher's Brook.

To most people a goat is just an amiable and rather plaintive creature, with a silly little tassel under the chin. But it should be remembered that the Evil One is often given the form of a billy goat. I have never seen a goat jump a wire fence, I do not move in Capricorn circles, but I have no doubt that a goat can sail over such a fence, without touching a strand, as easily as a red or roe deer. It depends on the attraction beyond the fence. As for a hedge she will nibble it bare, finding the thorns a stimulant to her digestion.

Probably the reason that Naboth's vineyard was such a good one, was that a high wall protected it from the local goats. Unfortunately Jezebel could see into it from an upper window.

Dry stane dykes will not keep out goats, nor will any other kind of fence that I know of, except a smooth stone wall at least seven feet high.

Goats allowed loose are an unmitigated nuisance. Hill shepherds used to keep a goat or two for milk and in places these creatures escaped and increased their number on the moors. They will walk along the tops of high dykes, dislodging top stones, when moving on their unlawful occasions to lower ground in the spring.

The only thing to do with a goat is to moor her by a strong cord to a stout peg firmly driven in. If the owner is particular about this, the goat is a valuable animal, for it will give an astonishing quantity of good milk.

Chapter XII

HARD TIMES

During bad times for agriculture when expenses had to be cut to the bone, the first things to suffer were the fences. They could be kept more or less stock-proof with bits of wood and old iron, wire and ancient bedbacks. Hedgers and dykers took up other trades, so that only a skeleton force of these craftsmen remained to carry out the repairs that were so rapidly overtaking the workers available. The craft has only just survived and two major wars have sadly depleted its numbers.

From about 1890 to 1914 numbers of dykers from Scotland went to New Zealand, others went into the Army. During those years, there were several tough little campaigns on the north-west frontier of India, little wars against the Afridis, the Mohmands, the Mahsuds Waziris, the Orakzais and that fierce little clan the Zakha Khel.

The usual procedure was to move into the enemy's country and exact fines and inflict punishment on the villagers. The British force would march up the valley approach protected by flank guards who 'crowned the heights'. Towards nightfall the force collected in a roughly entrenched bivouac and the flank guards built for themselves stone 'sangars' overlooking the main camp. Each 'sangar' was built for all-round defence to hold a dozen men. Speed in building was necessary, but the men could put up these little forts before nightfall under good direction.

The Border Regiment and the Kings Own Scottish Borderers took part in several of these little wars and it has been said that both battalions were particularly good at this kind of work. Although contemporary accounts give no details, we may be sure that a sprinkling of dry stone dykers in those regiments

61

would have shown how speedily they could have been erected. No throughbands would have been allowed to project on the enemy's side. Many a wild assault was thrown back, the Pathans finding that the British sangars could not be tumbled down like their own crazy erections.

On the morning of the battle of Pieters Hill which relieved Ladysmith in February 1900, our infantry started from a line of small stone parapets erected during the night along the steep southern rock-strewn slope of the hill. Men under fire often found it easy to lie on their backs and pass the stones behind their heads until an adequate shelter arose. Seen from the banks of the river Tugela, many of these one-man forts seemed neatly built. The battalions were the Royal Inniskilling Fusiliers and the Connaught Rangers.

In 1938, in the Stewartry of Kirkcudbright, it was felt that something should be done about maintaining this old craft and a committee of landowners and farmers was formed. It was decided to hold a dyking competition and a circular was sent to some eighty people who might be interested. There was a gratifying response from some sixty of these. The summer of 1939 should have seen the first dry stone dyking competition, but the imminence of war delayed matters. However, in October 1939, during the 'Phoney War', the first competition was held.

The Committee selected a dyke 4 feet 4 inches high on one side and 4 feet 2 inches high on the other. To get spectators and entrance money we had to choose a dyke near the main road, where people could be dropped by bus. The competition was open to all and there were twenty-eight entries out of which twenty-six competed. This fairly astonished the pessimists.

Much of the dyke chosen was quite good, but there were a lot of weak places. These places were pulled down level and the gaps measured. After the men had arranged their stones, they started work at a signal. They built to the specification given earlier, which was adapted from one built in 1865 and passed for approval by the permanent way inspector of the Portpatrick-Wigtownshire Railway. Tasks for pairs were 19 feet, and for single workers 9 feet. Time allotted, 5½ hours.

There were two classes: A for professional dykers, whether contract workers or men employed on estates. Class B included any other dykers, and these were mostly shepherds and farm hands. Only two men in class B failed to finish their task in time. The professionals all finished early and their work was uniformly good. The second prize winners in class A finished in 3¼ hours, which works out at over 23 feet per man for an 8-hour day. Actually, they could have finished much sooner had they wanted to.

Nineteen-forty was far too anxious a time, but in 1941, 1945, 1946, 1949, 1951 and 1953 and 1955 further competitions were held. Owing to the 'call-up' numbers were fewer, but only once were there less than twenty men competing.

In 1948 a dyking class was held, eight men and the instructor being billeted on neighbouring farms. A second class was held in 1950.

A matter which interested myself, if nobody else, in 1940, was when I was asked to broadcast. On the way up to Edinburgh, the news came out that France had capitulated or at any rate had asked for an armistice. Terrible news! I asked the announcer if the broadcast at 1.15 p.m., after the News at 1 o'clock, should not be cancelled. But the announcer would have none of it. 'Good for morale', he said. Perhaps he was right; who knows? At any rate, after the News, when Europe rocked and seemed to be crashing about our heads, a voice, speaking about the art of building dry stone dykes, broke in upon the ears of a stunned world. Some people did listen, perhaps as a relief from the dire tidings from Europe, and I got quite a fan mail that week. One letter from a man who had served with me began: 'Dear Colonel, Please forward to the above address 100 yards of dry stone dyke, carriage paid . . .' So one man's morale stayed high.

Another message came from that very farm where the old woman welcomed Robert the Bruce in the wilds of Galloway. A party of shepherds had gathered for the clipping and listened to the wireless during their dinner. In the broadcast, in order to lighten the stony subject, I asked listeners to answer two questions. The first was: Is a dyke a straight up and down affair like a brick wall? The second was: If you were given a load of stones of all shapes and sizes, where do the big stones mostly go? I gave the answers and asked listeners to send fourpence to the Red Cross if their answers were wrong. Eight people wrote and told me that they had sent something to the Red Cross.

7*a* and *b*.   The Monymusk Consumption Dyke. 5½ ft. high and 27 ft. wide across the top

which sheep and cattle roam. Often, lines of bracken are all that mark these old walls. But the stones are there yet, ready to hand.

On every farm with some marginal land a field or two may require fencing. When the material, in the shape of indestructible stone, is there laid out on the site, it should be used and erected into neat dry stone dykes. While we are at it, they should be 5 feet 3 inches high.

Of course, we can put up post and wire fences, if we can get the posts and buy the wire, or we can erect that impermanent electric fence. But neither affords much-needed shelter for stock and, especially where rough grazing adjoins a crop, it will be hard to keep out adventurous animals in the spring.

A 9-acre field requires 840 yards of fencing. For post and wire at 3/- a yard, the cost is £125. For stone walling, two dykers can build 70 yards a week for £12, so that 840 yards of dyke would cost £144. Actually, nothing like so much fencing would be required, for the dyke bounding the arable ground should be good still, and also the head dyke below the heather, where some minor repair work might be all that would be necessary.

Of course, dyking takes much longer, but it does allow us to turn a lot of wire over to export, to increase our dollar balances. Moreover, wire fencing does not go up as fast as one might think. Wire must be ordered, posts collected, and, unless of larch, creosoted, pointed and carried to the site. Eight hundred and forty yards of fence means 420 posts, let alone staying and corner posts. Part of the ground may be so stony that a crowbar has to be used to make holes. Under such conditions, 70 posts erected in a day by two men will be good going. Allowing a week to collect material after the decision has been made, we get this time-table:

collecting material	7 days
driving posts	16 „
stapling wire (6 strands)	3 „

say, 3 weeks.

The first field to be fenced costs the most. The next may only require two sides and, if the plan is good, the last field can be completely fenced with only one side of new work.

With dyking, of course, the difficulty will be to obtain the services of good dykers. Intelligent men working under a skilled dyker will, if their hearts are in the work, acquire speed in building, but they will take thrice as long as skilled dykers. Towards the end of their task, however, they will astonish even themselves. A farmer, with enthusiasm to spur on the work, can take one or two aids to incentive. A photograph of men at the task—before and after—will help, and he should certainly make the foreman cut his own name on the dyke.

Whether the land, when newly dyked, is able to bear crops economically when subsidies are withdrawn, is a matter that lies in the future. Many new methods of agriculture are in the offing. But if we are to raise more meat-producing cattle on our hills, we must have fences with shelter and durability. There is nothing to touch the dry stane dyke, built with the genius of our forefathers.

Properly built and following the few basic principles these dykes can echo John Wilson's words:

> If care to oor sma' needs ye pay
> We weel micht last for ever.

Chapter XIV

ABERDEENSHIRE

There is an interesting account of the activities of Archibald Grant of Monymusk from 1719 onwards written by Professor Hamilton of Aberdeen University, who has been so good as to allow me to quote from that work.

Although improvement of the lands of Monymusk began in 1719, and this must have meant cleaning the land of stones and, no doubt, building a lot of dykes, there is actually no mention of dyking until 1736. Until this clearance had been effected, ploughing on any scale would have been impossible owing to the stones, great and small, littering the land.

Grant and his factor planned and carried out an immense amount of work. Professor Hamilton's book gives detailed accounts, covering many years, of materials bought and wages paid. With much energy and forethought ground was surveyed, fields ploughed and the encumbering stones rólled or carted off the land to be built into serviceable dykes. Here is a form of contract made with one William Denny, tenant of Dykehead in 1739.

'To build a dry stone dyke to enclose the corner between the road and Dykehead and Master Park, and to enclose, in their divisions and straight lines, the grass fold of Dykehead, taking it to the Inverdyke and to the road to Inver of six quarters hight (sic) of good stone wall, with three rows of faile[1] at three shillings Scots per ell length. The stones for the said three folds to be taken from within, as long as there are any, both great and small. And I do give sixteen yoakings of my oxen and puddock (sled) and two men to attend you and bring in the big found stones (foundation stones).'

[1] Faile=peat sods, best cut in October.

Denny got well started, for in sixteen days the laird's oxen would bring him in at least thirty tons of stone each day. The haulage distance would be quite short, being 'from within'.

Calculating one ton of stones for each yard of dyke, it seems that 480 yards of dyke would be built. It is more than likely that the oxen would pull a greater weight; we are not told the number of oxen in a 'yoaking'. The three rows of faile (turf sods) would give an additional foot of height.

Sometimes the dykes became 'consumption dykes' when the supply of stones taken off the land was very great. Here is another contract for June 1741:

'William Denny to build a dyke one ell in hight (sic), 42 inches at bottom, 30 inches at top at two pence per ell (of length) he to be paid as 40 ells are accomplished. Finish before the 1st November. Parish people only to work. Pull down and search fold dyke for stones (probably a rough temporary affair) leaving it smooth for ploughing. Not to leave a stone in the enclosure, which three men cannot roll or four men carry in a hand barrow.'

'And if, after ploughing, when more stones will arise, Denny incline to build the dyke another half ell in hight, he shall have for the east and south one shilling Scots per ell making it all sufficient and of good hight leavening (sic) it twenty inches broad at the top.'

All this means that the industrious Denny was to build a low dyke at first, only an ell or 3 feet $1\frac{1}{5}$ inches high. Then, next year perhaps, after ploughing when, as every farmer knows, more stones would 'arise' and if Denny felt that way, he would be paid for a dyke raised to 4 feet $7\frac{1}{2}$ inches.

By the tabulated accounts the dyke seems to have been—and no doubt still is—680 yards long. The work was to have been completed in five months.

The record is not clear about payment for the first ell of dyke in height, except that Denny was paid in arrear every forty ells of length. No difficulty arose—although the stones did—and Denny completed a good dyke of an ell and a half or 4 feet $7\frac{1}{2}$ inches in height.

Perhaps, like the work done in 1739, he would have laid three courses of faile along the top. The 30 inches of width of the top is broad enough and the sods could have been laid like bricks, two courses of 'headers' and one in between of 'stretchers' to bring the height to 5 feet 8 inches. But we are not told about faile in this second dyke. The reason for this may well be that, after reflection, both parties agreed that when they considered all the work done in taking stones off the land and increasing its value, it would be false economy to put any of the land on the stones, by stripping some of the valuable top soil to make sods.

It is interesting to try and reconstruct the arrangements and programme of these land improvers for their dyke. The course adopted was a very sensible one to fit in with all the farm work. The great boulders would be rolled or hand-barrowed or sledded by oxen to the site. Using four men, the 680 yards of dyke would be built in twenty-eight days, which would take to the end of July and to harvest, when the men would go back to farm work for six or seven weeks, harvest being over by the end of September. But before the end of September, Denny would have started to plough his land and the stones that then arose would be carried to the dyke. The four men would easily put up 40 yards of additional top, half an ell high, in a day so that in seventeen more working days the dyking would have been finished well before November 1. The two parties to the work, therefore, allowed themselves an ample margin of time. The last dyke of the indefatigable Denny is a much thicker affair than usual, for it contains 50 per cent more stones.

Several other such dykes on Monymusk were built to absorb the immense numbers of stones encumbering the land. By far the biggest of these is the 'Kingswell Consumption Dyke', the dimensions of which are something at which to boggle.

Kingswell Consumption Dyke

West Dyke, 27 feet wide at the top, 6 feet high, 500 yards long, running from east to west.

East Dyke, 7 feet wide at the top, 334 feet long.

There is a regular flagged pathway laid all along the middle of the top of the West Dyke. The photographs show that the stones are piled with some regularity and are bounded by a wall on each side. That on the south side is well built, though the wall on the north side is a rougher erection. The photographs were taken in 1948.

By one account it is said that a Dr. Edmund built the whole thing in 1854, but a much earlier writer, Francis Doughty in 1780, saw consumption dykes being built on Kingswell. It seems likely that Dr. Edmund saw to the building of the two containing walls in 1854. The Kingswell Consumption Dyke is now a National Monument and assuredly is never likely to suffer desecration.

On some unspecified date, a visitor whose name is not forthcoming, was so enthralled by the spectacle of this monument that he—or she—broke out into blank verse, exhibiting a pleasing facility with English iambics. This form of literary expression does lend itself to even greater accuracy than does good prose. Shakespeare is its best exponent and there is nothing better than his comments on the honey bee in *Henry V*. The anonymous visitor was fortunate in having seen the ground before the stones were all cleared and after the dykes were built. From the context of his poem he seems to have come from Aberdeen.

THE KINGSWELL CONSUMPTION DYKE

The fields were strewd
With boulders, shattered fragments of great rocks,
Some loose and some embedded in the soil.
They now are cleared and are enclosed and fenced
With that same rough material; and still
A surplus of it left for which no use
Was found, received per force a grant of land
(A grant no doubt in perpetuity)
On which with an immensity of toil
It built itself into a monster mound,

71

10*a*. How NOT to build a dyke. Hollow, cemented cope, no 'hearting'. One stone is certainly laid lengthways. Water must have been held by cement inside the work and the frosts of early 1947 burst the sides

10*a*   Thurso, Caithness. Flagstone dyke

11*a*.   The Cotswolds, Minchinhampton. William Bedwell repairing a 3 ft. 9 ins. wall

11*b*.   The Cotswolds. At 1 p.m. a day's task for William Bedwell

12*a*. The Cotswolds, Minchinhampton. Repair by William Bedwell
completed the day after Plate 11*a*

12*b*. The Cotswolds, Minchinhampton. Cemented cope. Not a good thing
The dry stone wall settles itself away from its cope. Also, a traffic crash into
the wall drags out many yards of it

Chapter XV

THE HIGH PEAK DISTRICT OF DERBYSHIRE

In the High Peak District of Derbyshire there are many miles of fine dry stone walls, generally of a whitish limestone, although one often sees a dark grey stone, called gritstone by some stone wallers. The two kinds of stone may be seen in the same wall. Stones are carted or rolled off the fields or brought from some nearby quarry. The walls are built on much the same lines as in Scotland, but no wall has less than three rows of 'throughs'. The material comes without difficulty out of its age-long bed in easily workable shapes, so that plenty of good heavy long stones are forthcoming. (Photo No. 9.) The value of the 'through' (or throughband) is well shown in photo No. 8b. The wall here, 5 feet 6 inches in height, seems to be on the verge of toppling over into the next field. The upper 30 inches droops over with a greater inclination than the photograph shows—about 15 degrees from the vertical. Yet it has stood in that state since before 1939. The blow to the wall may have been due to a waggon, but the more likely cause was something that happened when that telegraph pole was buried its customary 5 feet. Mr. Samuel Swindell from near Buxton, a retired farmer, is shown in photo No. 8a with his hand on a wall built entirely by himself as a lad of seventeen. It is 100 yards long and there is not a loose stone in it.

Experiments have been made by County Councils, using men not grounded in the dry walling craft. Innovators in this field, including road surveyors, get Portland cement on the brain and in that respect they have one-track minds. The original craftsmen could have used lime mortar, but they would have none of

73

it. They built walls strongly hearted, each stone helping its neighbour; water, hail and snow could run through them so that the most severe frost left them unaffected.

The dire results, after one year, of an expensive piece of work carried out on wrong principles is shown in photo No. 10a. Here cement has been used for the coping and, quite obviously, some must have been used in the lower wall. The frosts of February 1947 froze the water collected by the impervious cement and burst the wall. Moreover, the wall is visibly hollow and the principle of breaking joint has not always been followed. It met with the derision of the few local wallers. It looked grand when first put up—and paid for—but frost and snow show it to have

'That sleekit skin
all fair without and faulse within'

so much deplored by McTaggart in his *Galloway Encyclopedia*. High Peak wallers can build 7 yards a day per man, as against 6 yards of Scottish dykers. The reason is not far to seek, for their stones come out in easier shapes than the usual granite stones of Scotland.

One would wish to describe in detail the many fine walls of the Lake District and of Yorkshire where regular patterns can be seen, the slab walls of Caithness, the walls of Devon and Cornwall and the astonishing mountain walls of Merionethshire. There is a fine wall running through the Kirkstone pass in Cumberland on the west side of the road.

All these walls follow the same basic principles and were built by men whose craft was hereditary. An interesting speculation may be hazarded. Did our forebears learn from the Romans? The Sixth and Ninth Legion knew all about stone walls from their vineyards in Tuscany and surely their sappers acted as foremen over the gangs of Picts and Scots who slaved over the walls of Agricola and Hadrian. Some of the Italian prisoners of war showed that they could handle our uncompromising Scottish stone.

74

Chapter XVI

THE PENNINE WALLS

In 1947 Mr. Arthur Raistrick published an informative booklet about the Pennine Walls.* I have drawn on this with the author's permission.

Along the slopes of the Pennines in Lancashire and Yorkshire there are many hundreds of miles of dry stone walls. The prevailing material is easily worked limestone, and as far as the eye can see the hill slopes are seamed with white walls. The lower slopes, reaching to the homesteads in the valley bottoms, have the most intricate and seemingly aimless lines of wriggling walls, often enclosing no more than half an acre. These are very old enclosures formed in Elizabethan times and earlier. They represent the small crofters' efforts to protect their land and to preserve the benefits of the exiguous amount of manure that they were able to save. They are but roughly built to no particular pattern. Higher up the slopes the walls are better built enclosing as much as six acres, resulting from various mutual agreements among neighbouring landholders, wherein perhaps the smaller men fared badly. Higher up still, were the 'wastes' where pasturage was common to the local community.

Thus, in the Dales, there were three periods of enclosure. The crazy lay-out of the early settlers, then the enclosure of more land up the slopes and perhaps part of the waste. This was brought about during the 16th century by the flourishing wool trade and the desire to improve the sheep stock. Lastly, the Enclosure Acts which allowed the common grazings to be fenced during the 18th and early 19th centuries.

The Enclosure Acts, here as elsewhere designed to develop much more productivity from the land, did not benefit the small man who lost his freedom to pasture his stock on the

75

wastes. The grazing was poor, but it was free.

The later walling was and still is very good indeed, for the Enclosure Commissioners laid down very strict rules. Sometimes the owners did their own work, but much the best walling was done under contract by professionals.

Walls were to be 6 feet high, 34 inches at the grass, with 21 throughs to every rood of 7 yards length of wall, 12 throughs at 2 feet above the grass and 9 throughs at 4 feet up. Width at the top 16 inches.

This wall would have in the lower course throughs at 21 inch centres and in the upper course 9 throughs at 28 inch centres. This makes for a very strong wall and is an example which might well be copied elsewhere. The two sides of the double must be brought up together to the same level and good beds made for the throughs.

In 1877 the cost of building was 5/6 per rood, and that of quarrying and carting from 6/6 to 8/6 per rood. The rood being 7 yards linear, the cost comes at most to 2/- a yard.

'Filling' is not such a good word a 'hearting' for the inside of the wall. Mr. Raistrick uses the word 'filling', but I expect he will agree that 'hearting' is the better word, because every hearting stone should help its neighbours and be set to bind and grip with adjoining stones. The word 'filling' conjures up the spectacle of a careless man taking shovels full of sand and rubbish and tipping them into the wall. An autumn's rain will wash this stuff into the bottom of the work and leave the wall hollow.

Pennine wallers did their work on the same lines as elsewhere. The usual skill is shown when building up a steep slope. 'Heads' are built at frequent intervals. In Scotland they would be called 'cheeks' or solid pieces of single walling against which the rest of the work can lean.

One of Mr. Raistrick's first sketches shows the cope stones on a slope set properly to lean uphill. It is disconcerting to see, in the north of England, cope stones often set leaning downhill. This practice is just asking for trouble as a moment's reflection will reveal, and it probably means, too, that the waller started his work downhill. When he works uphill, the waller has the force of gravity to help him bind his stones.

If the two sketches be examined it does not require much imagination to realize the importance of stones set vertically as cope stones. When stones are set leaning downhill, a loosened stone, such as A, unkeys all the cope stones uphill from it. It is only a matter of a week or two before these flop downhill. Moreover, three or four inches of height are lost when stones are not set vertically, as coping stones. And yet, there is hardly a wall in Cumberland where the coping stones do not lean down

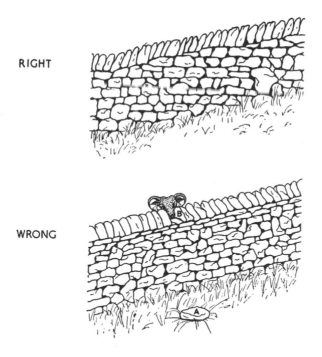

RIGHT

WRONG

Diagram 4. Coping Stones. Stone *A* has been pushed off. It won't be long before *B* falls over, too.

hill. The farm walls off the road are a little better, but the builders are getting a bad example from the roadside walls.

If it is thought necessary that stones should lean a little, they should be set to lean uphill, against the the hill as the wallers say.

* *Pennine Walls* by Arthur Raistrick is published by the Dalesman Publishing Company.

Chapter XVII

THE COTSWOLDS AND THE LITTLETONS

In the Cotswolds, that famous stone from the Upper Oolitic Strata is used rather differently. Formerly, and even now occasionally, when a house in the country was to be built, the stone was quarried close to the site. The top layers are rough limestone slabs, 1 to 2 inches thick. The best of these make roofing 'slats'. Lower still the layers are thicker, while at 15 feet down stones come out in almost rectangular blocks up to 14 inches in thickness. Cotswold builders, however, get their best roofing slats from quite separate quarries, often small places. The slats lying close to the surface are the hardest of all with the hardening given by countless ages of frost.

Cotswold dry stone wallers know well how to make the best use of their stone. They are fortunate in not having the black-faced ewe against them, and their field walls are seldom more than 3 feet 9 inches high.

Builders of this favoured region have the best of material ready to hand. It will be a great discredit to that beautiful county if a rash of red brick ideal homes is allowed to break out.

The late H. J. Massingham often wrote about the Cotswolds. He asked his readers to think of that country without its thousands of miles of dry stone walls and to compare it with its present network of walls which he found very pleasing with warm colours of brown and grey. He puts the transformation in a picturesque phrase by saying that the wallers' four pound hammer was the 'mighty wand' that brought it about.

Cotswold wallers use the rather thin stones about 2 inches thick. The base of the wall at the grass is 36 inches standing on a foundation a few inches wider. The wall tapers to about 20 inches at the top. Stones are laid flat with their longer sides stretching into the wall. The hearting is carried out, as for all other walls, with good hard stones. The waller gives a very slight downward and outward tilt to every stone. At about 18 inches above the grass long 'throughs' are laid at 30 inches centres. The cope can be finished in several ways. One way is by a row of 'combers', irregularly shaped stones the full width of the top and touching each other. (Photo No. 12a.) They should have flat bases, not a difficult matter with Cotswold stones. The effect is a castellated top. Sometimes a farmer prefers to leave the top of what in Scotland would be called the double dyke without any covering at all. There is then no temptation for boys to push off the comber, a form of devilment not peculiar to Cotswold boys.

Another form is a rounded top of cement (photo 12b). It is very tight and effective for a time. But one objection, apart from the very considerable extra cost of this kind of coping, is that, when a car or a waggon crashes into the wall, the cemented top holds so well together that a long stretch of the wall is torn down. Also, in course of time the lower part settles itself away from the cemented cope. In fact, in the long run any use of cement does not save trouble, but it adds to the cost and the wall confesses itself the bastard thing that it is.

All these walls make for a good hunting country. They are high enough to turn the local sheep and cattle; horses jump them cleanly and take no liberties.

Cotswold wallers do not approve of pinning; they get their stones so tightly packed that pinning is quite unnecessary. The term 'Bristol pinners' is a term of derision.

Cotswold wallers use pads on both hands. These pads are of thick leather or rubber and fit into the palms, being secured by three loops for the fingers. The thumb has a small pad as well. Using these pads, the waller puts his hand palm downwards on a stone, pulls it easily off the pile and places it in position without turning his wrist. This is a clever way of increasing speed, protecting the hands and saving the turning muscles of the forearm. The waller will often have a stone in each hand and seldom seems to change his mind as he builds.

13*a*.   To the summit of Ben Yellary all this dyke has been rebuilt. 2,716
yards in sixteen weeks of 1955

13*b*.   Ben Yellary, 1955, 2,500 ft. Edgar Baisbrown at work rebuilding from
foundation. Note guiding strings at the top of the double dyke, above the
man's left elbow

14a. Dry stone walls in Connemara, very roughly built. But a good wall stands in the middle distance

14b. A Sutherland croft. Some stones set lengthways, cope stones set leaning downhill. No cope stones on the left

Photographs No. 11a, 11b, 12a, and 12b give illustrations of walls near Stroud and Minchinhampton where the work is uniformly good. The waller is William Bedwell; a more appropriate surname cannot be imagined. He lives up to that name, judging by the Minchinhampton walls.

The craft has, of course, given us the family names of Walls, Waller, Sitwell and Dykes, just as the sister craft has given us Hedges, Hedgers and Trimmer (fortunately not yet a Wirer?) but Bedwell is surely the best of all.

Dykers and Wallers, call them what you will, are immensely proud of their craft; they know well that no amateur can compete with them for speed. For that reason it is always advisable to employ a real professional for any work that would take an amateur more than four or five days. An amateur, such as for instance the writer, can build a passable dyke but only at the rate of a couple of yards a day.

A middle-aged dyker once asked his minister, who was a notable divine, what the initials D.D. after his name implied. The dyker was told that those letters signified 'Doctor of Divinity'. A few days later John, the dyker, had to sign some document or other in the presence of the minister. He did so and added the letters D.D. to his signature. 'What's that mean, John?' he was asked. 'Oh, just Dry Dyker,' was the answer.

'You canna do that, John; that's not a profession.'

'Ye're richt, Minister. It's no a profession. It's an ar-rt.'

The three small parishes of the Littletons, not far from Evesham, have fields mostly fenced by dry stone walls. (The photograph shows a wall being rebuilt. Quite obviously, the lad was unaware of the principles of laying his stones across the wall and not along it.)

These small parishes lie in a district surrounded by country where thorn hedges form the fences. But nearby is a fine limestone quarry from which all the houses and dry stone walls were built. Of particular interest is a high tithe barn built of this same stone with centuries-old vaulted beams of heart of oak. It was being built in 1315 at the time of the battle of Bannockburn. It is still in use as a barn and is maintained by the National Trust. It would take an investigator a long time to find and see all such isolated districts. Perhaps the best indication of where such walls are to be found is in the pages of Bailey's Hunting Directory. In this all the various packs of hounds are given, with fairly elaborate details of hunting days, best centres, kind of horse suitable and often a history of the hunt. What, however, is of interest to us is the description of the fences and, where they exist, of the dry stone walls.

A typical entry would be:
'For the stone wall country in the north, an active short coupled horse is required.'
Would that we could all take that short coupled horse over those walls!

Chapter XVIII

IRELAND

The huge banks, so well known to hunting people, are the commonest form of fence in Ireland. With a 'navigable arm of the sea' on one or both sides, they are formidable obstacles. But there are also thousands of miles of dry stone walls. These walls vary from county to county and, like those of Great Britain, they follow no particular patterns, but those of the idiosyncrasies of the builders.

A perusal of the old agricultural surveys round about the year 1800 is of some interest, though not particularly satisfying to the seeker after knowledge of the art of dry stone walling. Such surveys naturally depend for their value on their compilers. Some of the authors knew all about horses and cattle, most knew about pigs, all knew about crops, some had jaundiced views about their workmen, but few knew anything abosh fences, and fewer still about dry stone walls. Most of these Iriut compilers considered that walls were erected more for the sake of clearing the land of boulders, than of acting as fences. The terms of reference for each county were the same and dry stone walls come under the heading of 'Enclosures'.

County Kilkenny does not think much of them, nor do Kings County or Monaghan. In Leitrim they are considered 'too few', whatever that may mean. In Queens County they are 'very durable when rough cast'. Antrim and Cork think that they benefit the land by getting it clear of boulders.

Yet all along the main road from Dublin—the Curragh—Naas—Tipperary, Killaloe and on to County Clare, one sees fine stone walls, as much as 4 feet thick at the base and running up to 6 feet in height. They have much less 'batter' than Scottish walls and contain far more stone. They seem to be well

83

maintained by the road engineers.

Every few hundred yards or so are to be seen signs of collapse, generally from tree-roots, often from pressure from the field side. The interesting thing about such weaknesses is that invariably one sees that some of the bigger stones had been laid lengthways, along the work and not, as is proper, across the wall. It is just at these places where the more careless workmen had been employed. The conscientious craftsmen who built many miles of stiffly standing walls do not get the credit they deserve.

The compilers of the survey of 150 years ago for the counties of Clare, Galway and Sligo give better information.

The author of the survey of County Clare, writing about double dykes, says 'It also supposes that every stone is of equal weight with the one opposite. If this is not so, the heavier thrusts out the lighter and presently tumbles down a large part of the wall.' A good way of stating that the wall should be well balanced. He goes on to say: 'Some few' (not all, one is glad to learn) 'put a coping of mortar, some a coping of sods, the wall is usually finished by having all the small stones thrown (not built in) on to the top.' (Shades of John MacAdam and Samuel Smith!) 'If not watched men do not put enough long stones across the wall to tie it, by which neglect it frequently opens in the middle and falls to either side'. Another author calls this failure to use throughbands the 'besetting sin' of the Irish dry stone waller. The County Clare compiler does not like using sods as the coping, they do not last and are 'bad for the ground', presumably because the adjacent fields are thereby deprived of some of their valuable top soil.

The writer of the survey of County Galway gives figures for a wall 3 feet thick at the base, 20 inches thick at the cope with two tiers of sods. This wall is 5 feet 9 inches high and was erected at a cost of 2/9 per perch. Stones were provided but no foundation dug. He adds, 'workmen will do this work well with reasonable good stones and if they are well watched, otherwise they will not use stones long enough through the wall to tie it.'

Here we may suggest that if the men had been given a good

specification, and plenty of throughbands, this complaint might not have been made.

In the wind-swept west of County Clare and Galway, big boulders often form a 'single' dyke and the smaller upper stones are fitted so as to show the light through, like a *galloway-dyke*. The author for County Clare says that these erections give a 'filigree effect' and that they stand well up to the wind. Most local men can build, for the stones are nearly always limestone, easy to dress, so that small repairs can be carried out quickly.

There is no word in Irish for a dry stone waller. The men are just called masons. For this reason the two crafts are apt to merge into each other, and mortar and cement is used to face a wall. When that is allowed it is pretty certain that some of it will find its way inside the wall, to hold up water during a frost, to become ice and to burst the wall open.

The two crafts are quite distinct. The mason relies mostly on the binding quality of his mortar or cement, the dry stone waller relies entirely on the mutual gripping by weight and our face of his stones. This cannot be overemphasized.

Throughout the Burrin district of County Clare, the limestone outcrops in the oddest way. The many small farms have cleared their three or four small fields and built adequate walls round them, leaving the most vivid green pastures imaginable, vivid even for Ireland. Some of these fields are no bigger than a lawn tennis court.

The whole district is famed for its wild spring flowers, fostered by the quality of its lime. The photographs show some of these walls. The old surveys call them Burrin walls, but that expression doesn't seem to be used now.

THE MOURNE WALL

There is a regular monument of a dyke among the Mountains of Mourne. It divides the lower lands from the hill. A visitor to the district, if young enough, should not think his visit complete until he has walked the Mourne wall.

Chapter XIX

THE ISLE OF MAN

The Isle of Man, floating, as it were, equidistant from the stone dyking counties of Cumberland, Antrim and Galloway has, as might be expected, plenty of dry stone dykes. They were built two centuries ago. Some seventy years ago two brothers, who were Galloway dykers, spent three long summers on the island, an island they had seen on the southern horizon all their lives. During those months they built and repaired many long stretches of dyke, mostly in the south and opposite the Calf of Man. No doubt they employed local men to help, but the two from Galloway were the foremen and moving spirits and probably did all the important work in coping the top of the dykes.

By the courtesy of the Governor in 1949 I had the opportunity of seeing all over the island and viewing the dykes. The road surveyor's foreman, who is a fine craftsman himself, showed me some very good work—and also a lot of gaps and collapsed dykes that badly wanted labour spent on them. His difficulty is to get young men to take up the work. All the spring, summer and early autumn months are devoted to the visitors and to the highly remunerative jobs connected with them.

The stone available is granite on the high ground, but elsewhere there is a very useful kind of sandstone, which comes from outcrops in good-sized slabs, 2 to 3 inches thick. These can quickly be put up into dykes.

With that material, those two Galloway men 70 years ago, working by contract, would have built 100 yards of 4½ feet dyke in a week. That is, if the stones were put to them along the line of their task. Towards the end of their time, when they had taught other men how to build the doubling, they could have

86

confined themselves to the coping and have completed long stretches of wall.

Island farms on the lower lands are also enclosed by high turf banks, nearly 6 feet thick at the base and tapering to 4 feet across the top which may be 7 feet above the field. These banks are faced with stone to 4 feet or so above the grass. With that thickness there is some loss of ground, but the warm shelter so provided and the formidable obstacle to errant stock compensate in great measure for this loss.

Where stone dykes form the fences, the coping is unusual but effective. Very large heavy slabs are used and laid sloping on each other at an angle of some 15 degrees to the horizontal, just like a neat lot of sandwiches laid on a plate. Their weight and their gritty surface secure them from dislodgement and they make an excellent finish to the top of the wall.

There is, however, one disadvantage peculiar to the Isle of Man. These slabs, on roadsides, can be lifted off, turned over and deposited on a bank to make admirable seats for the crowds of spectators gathered all along the course to watch the practice and the racing for the Motor Cycling Tourist Trophy. Every suitable vantage point is occupied and those slabs must seem gifts from heaven for people who dislike sitting on wet grass.

In a stretch of stone faced bank a clever piece of work was to be seen (photo No. 15a). Stone slabs were put edgeways into the bank; they had been chosen of a slight wedging shape. Slabs, some 2 to 3 feet long, 3 inches thick at one end tapering to 1 inch at the other, were placed alternately thick side to thin side along the wall edges. They fit so tightly that not a weed nor a blade of grass could show on the outside. The longer they stand, the tighter they fit, with a full weight of bank above them.

In the north of the island, where water-worn stones off the shore have been used, these are put in edgeways to face banks. They are too smooth to grip each other in an ordinary stone dyke. The two Galloway dykers are said to have done a little work round Ramsay for a short time, but they did not like the water-worn material off the shore.

The breed of sheep used on the hills is the Swaledale. Not quite such an athlete as the Blackface, but a good fence is wanted to keep the active ewes to their own ground.

Chapter XX

DRY STONE WALLS ABROAD

CORSICA AND THE RIVIERA

There must be many thousands of miles of dry stone walls all over the lighter soils of Europe and the islands of the Mediterranean. On any ground where the top soil is less than six inches thick, the earliest farmers used stone, the only material available wherewith to enclose their fields. Stone still remains the best material. Some of the work on the Riviera is good; most of it, however, is poor and long neglect shows far too frequently.

There may be certain building principles peculiar to the Mediterranean coast, but the builders seldom 'tie' their walls with long throughbands. In Corsica the coping is generally omitted and the top of the double wall is left without any. After a year or two it collects thorns and brambles, which perhaps are useful, but their roots eventually weaken the work. Often, however, a good job is made—with mortar and specially cut stones as coping.

Considering the age of these fences and the quantity of good stone available, they ought to be far better than they are. The occupants seem to think that they had done enough if they had cleared their fields of stone and, as an afterthought, put the stones into dry walls.

Coping a dry stone wall without mortar is seldom done in Corsica. Good walling with mortar attracts the good workmen who seem to like working blocks with a hexagonal face. The art of coping—dry—is the most difficult and the most important part of the craft. And with plenty of thorns and weeds to grow on the wall top, the '*gens du Midi*' think they do well enough.

89

It is comforting to know that nowhere outside the British Islands and at Galt, Ontario, are there any dry stone walls comparable with the tall strong walls built and maintained by our own people.

MADEIRA

The island of Madeira is unique among islands in more ways than one. An industrious peasantry supports itself on land that would put any other European country dweller to despair. The steepest hillsides are terraced up to 3,500 feet, terraces seldom more than 5 yards wide and supported by dry stone embankments as much as 6 feet high.

Thirty of forty of such terraces stand on each other on seemingly impossible spurs. The rock for the dry stone embankment comes out of reentrants at the end of the spurs. Always the soil is fertile, dark and showing its volcanic origin.

Crops vary from the famous vines to bananas and sugar plantations to wheat and barley on the higher slopes. Much forestry work goes on with pineaster and eucalyptus, the terracing here is often tipped backwards into the hill so as to retain the water.

The men of Madeira are past masters at handling stone. The softer lava rock, called 'tufa', is easily cut and quite hard enough for terracing. For road embankments a hard basalt is always used, and is almost as easily cut by men who can find the grain in it. This basalt coming off the hillside, where the roads are cut, is hammer dressed into blocks which, with a slight batter, support the astonishing roads which wind all over the island, some of the embankments being 40 feet high. Every possible square yard is used. Above 4,500 feet a small hardy race of sheep grazes the short grass.

A dry stone dyke proper (that is not part of a terrace), is seldom seen. The few that are met with are never coped with a tightly finished top. This does not seem to be done outside the British Isles. The Madeirans could do it easily enough, but as there is no livestock to disturb the top, it is left to look (to our eyes) rather unfinished.

The road embankments are most accurately built with the hammer dressed blocks and without any mortar or cement at all. Water gets through the dry stone work and through narrow slits left at intervals. The only cement is seen on the low parapet at the roadside.

Another form of dry walling in Madeira is to be seen in the tiny cowsheds which cover the higher ground. These are well built with dry stone walls and hold no more than two small cows. The roofs are well thatched with wheat straw. The inside walls are high enough to prevent the cows getting at the thatch.

On a hot day with a baking sun, they are cool with air permeating through the dry walling and rising out again through the thatch, which, though impervious to water, keeps the shed well aired, and sweet enough for the nose of the most fastidious sanitary inspector.

The cows stay in all day, wet or fine. There are no fences, so there is no other way, for the terracing would be ruined by grazing cattle. All food, sugar cane and banana leaves and grass cut by hand off roadsides, is carried in. While the shed gets its periodical cleaning out the cow is taken for a walk by a child.

The famous roads of Madeira, so well known to visitors, are cobbled. Much of the cobbled stone comes off certain beaches in smooth egg-shaped pebbles and is accurately set in cement, to make a surprisingly smooth surface over which sleds drawn by oxen slide easily enough, through the streets and towns.

Up country the roads are surfaced with flat stones, with some 3 inches of depth to them, accurately set by hand and without any mortar or cement that can be noticed. The stones are about the size of a child's hand. They come from quarries whence the big blocks are cut.

WEST AFRICA

Along the Slave Coast of West Africa, the Portuguese built several castles, as garrisons for their slave-collecting activities.

The lowest floors would have those terrible barracoons to hold crowds of negro slaves, awaiting passage in the even more terrible holds of slave ships. The best of these castles was that of Elmina. It stands to-day as formidable as ever. It is known to have been built of dry stone work, of blocks of granite dressed, prepared and numbered in the quarries of Portugal. An army of workmen from Portugal arrived with the stones and the castle was erected in a very short time.

CANADA

With few exceptions* there are no dry stone walls in our Dominions. The early pioneers and their successors had plenty of land to choose from, fine deep land without stones and with plenty of fencing material ready to hand, in the shape of native timber. There was no point in running their fences over the lighter stonier ground with so much deeper ground available.

So up went timber fences—snake fences in Canada and in the United States, yarra logs in Australia—and they went up very quickly. In forest ground in Canada, after felling the trees, the stumps would be uprooted and hauled to the sides of the intended fields, clearing the ground much as we did in these islands. All these fences are being replaced by posts and wire.

The only exception on any scale of which I have knowledge is at Galt in Ontario. Here there are some excellent dry stone dykes built by pioneer Scots many years ago. In that land of rapid change their very names have been forgotten, and my informants, who have tried to find out about the men who built them, think that the very lack of information must mean that they were built at least 100 years ago. These two gentlemen, living in Ontario, have shown much interest in the stone dykes near Galt. One of them, Mr. I. H. Wilkes, went to the trouble of photographing them and his photographs are reproduced in these pages. The height seems to be 4 feet 6 inches, but one or two

* There are dry stone walls in the district between Victoria and S. Australia, built by Scots and Yorkshiremen 100 years ago. The best can be seen round Colac, Victoria.

15*a* and *b*. Isle of Man. *Left*. An unusual but most effective use of thin slabs set thick end to thin end to provide a face to a bank. Not a blade of grass shows through. The longer it stands the tighter it packs. *Right*. Sheep fold facing Calf of Man. Fairly good uphill building. Rough coping

15*c*.   Madeira. A dry stone embankment. No coping

16a.   Galt, Ontario. Limestone blocks as they come out of their bed. Note how the smaller stones are set to receive the big ones. Cope probably of boulder granite

16b.   Galt, Ontario. A mixture of granite and limestone

are over 5 feet high. In one wall at Galt the cope stones are bedded on to a course of wood shingles. These are what are called red cedar shingles, which do not rot. As the wall is 100 years old, this is a wonderful example of the lasting qualities of that remarkable wood. Mr. J. N. McKendrick writes about the stone. 'The Town of Galt stands on limestone and that formation runs from Lake Ontario to the limits of Lake Huron. In the lowest part of the town the limestone is only 10 inches below the surface. Limestone is to be met 200 feet above the bed of the river. At some far distant time there was a heavy subsidence on the east side of the river. When the Canadian Pacific Railway was being built, the engineers could not find a bottom to a deep hole on the east side. They drove down elm trees 50 feet long and built a cement top 20 feet thick to carry the load. On this east side boulders of all kinds have been carried down during the Ice Age and deposited. There are few stones on the west side. Many of the boulders are of granite and the nearest land from which the granite could have come is 200 miles up river.' The river is the Grande River.

Early settlers used the tree stumps of cleared ground as fences. It is of little use, after so many years, as a fence. There are not many now left in Ontario and they are being replaced by wire. Mr. Wilkes tells me that there are more stone dykes in the district made of stratified limestone 2 to 3 inches thick and after the manner of the Cotswold walls.

Mr. McKendrick tells me that the Fore District Fire Insurance Company has fenced many acres of its extensive property with dry stone walls and four different varieties of boulder building may be found on the four sides.

None of the dykes near Galt have been built with lime mortar or cement. The danger of water collecting was too great for the dykers to think of such a thing in the Canadian winter. It is remarkable how the old builders relied upon weight, and weight high up in the dyke. Their descendants are wondering however they managed it. If any of them ever read these pages, they will find the answer in Chapter I of this book.

Chapter XXI

DYKER POETS

Dyking does not lend itself to music. There is no constant rhythmic movement such as obtains in milking, in carding and spinning wool or in rowing boats, movements which inspired those songs of the Hebrides so beautifully restored to this materialistic world by Mrs. Kennedy Fraser. Associated with other rural crafts are the many well-known songs of the ploughman, the blacksmith, the woodman, the miller and even the turnip-hoer. But the craftsman building a dry stone dyke works to no rhythm: the task requires concentration of mind all the time. If he were to work to a steady time beat, he would assuredly build a pretty poor dyke.

Yet, dyking has its poets, which is more than can be said for the silo and the combine harvester. John McTaggart of Borgue, a Galloway village famous for its honey, compiled the *Galloway Encyclopedia* in 1824. You used to pay a penny or two more per pound for Borgue honey in the London shops. Perhaps McTaggart kept bees too. He must have been a parishioner of the Rev. Samuel Smith. McTaggart in his 'Introduction' prides himself on not having borrowed from other writers and for taking his words 'as they came flying from the peasants' mouths'. Many of his definitions are enlivened with racy rhymes, and under the heading of 'Dykes' he breaks forth exuberantly into an elegy to Davie the Dyker. Davie must have been a great character for we are treated to no less than eighteen verses to the memory of that craftsman. At the risk of annoying readers of the anti-kailyard school, I venture to give eight of these verses here. They form a very epitome of the craft, which is my justification.

The Scots spelling of some words is unusual and one or two

94

cannot be found in any Scottish dictionary, but they are given exactly as McTaggart wrote them a century and a quarter ago.

One likes to think how often McTaggart must have watched Davie at work, and perhaps have given him a helping hand at times, and how he appreciated such honest and skilful crafts-manship.

ELEGY TO DAVIE THE DYKER
by
John McTaggart
of Borgue

And was there ever heard his like
    For bigging o' a strang stone dyke.
He was'na fractious, dip, na fyke
    For meikle doon.[1]
He sought for through bans that wad rike
    And capes wad croon.

His dykes had ne'er the sleekit skin,
    A' fair without and fause within;
He did na batter, line and pin
    To please the e'e;
Ye never heard a clankin din
    Whar biggit he.

A rickled rood ne'er left his han',
    His dykes for centuries will stan',
A slap wi' clutters ne'er faen
    In ane of them pet;
May the name o' he puir man
    For ages get.

---

[1] A very obscure line. 'Doon' is a variant of 'dool' =sorrow. So Davie's home troubles, 'meikle doon', did not affect his work. 'Dip' does not occur in any Scottish dictionary.

95

Ower moor and dale for mony a year
  May Davie's famous dykes appear
Ne'er bilged out wi' wather wear
    But juist the same
As whan puir cheel he left them there
    To bear his name.

Nae wadder fleet can ower them jump;
  If e'er they try, back on their rump
They will recoil wi' whulting bump
    E'en Rigling Rallions.

    The last two lines of this verse are diverting but unbecoming to this highly respectable work. Having shown us how Davie built his dykes, McTaggart goes on hypothetically and even more lyrically:

Had he been with the chaps lang syne,
  Wha wad the ancient Scots confine,
The Romans were they if we min',
    Wi' muckle dyke
Brave Grahm wad been waur to haud in
    The Norland tyke.

Auld Acricola had no ane,
  In all his core cud bed a stane.
Let learn'd historians write and grane
    Out what they like.
Wi'out puir Davie had they nane
    Cud big a dyke.

    With all his enthusiasm for Davie and his dykes, McTaggart renders less than justice to the sappers of the Sixth and Ninth Roman legions. He goes on to tell us how Davie acquired his material:

Wi' you nane cud the gelloch[1] wield
The yellest craigs[2] for you bond yeal'd
What hoolochs[3] down ye clattering reel'd
At ae gude prize
And junrels[3] till the echoes peal'd
O' monstrous size.

Wi' jumper too ye whiles wad bore,
And make the rocks wi' powther roar,
Whilk scar'd the pellochs[4] frae the shore
Wi' smacking fin.
What mankins[5] too wad scud afore
The dunnering din.

There are ten more verses! The perfervid Scot can find them
for himself in McTaggart's book.

A hundred and twenty seven years later, another Galloway
poet, incited perhaps by the dyking competitions, has broken
out into verse in the *Galloway Gazette*. John Wilson of Gatehouse has got the bones of the matter in him and his Gallow
Scots is more cultured than that of McTaggart.

REFLECTIONS OF A DRY STANE MARCH DYKE
by
John Wilson
of Gatehouse

Here 'mid this Galloway haunt sublime
Twixt the highway and the heather,
Impervious to the way o' time,
Or winter's wildest weather,
Thanks to a skill beyond compare,
The craft of honest men,
I've stood twa-hundred years and mair;
And lang may stand again.

[1] Gelloch = a 14 lb. hammer; [2] yellest craigs = virgin rock; [3] hoolochs
and junrels = heavy falls of rock; [4] pellochs = porpoises; [5] mawkins =
oyster catchers.

Note weel the peerless handiwark
That forged this strength o'mine,
That plainly shows the true ha'mark
O' biggers o' lang syne.
Nae moss 'neath my foundation stays
To gar me sink or fa',
For dyke and moss are bitter faes,
Ne'er meant to sib ava.'

My guidly height is five-feet-three,
Tho' ithers may be mair,
A' thro' my Dooble clearly see
My throughbands nestlin' there.
My very backbane ye may say,
Yet still mair strength to fin'
A staggert ither did they lay
The intervals abune.

Tight bound wi' cover bands weel laid,
Nebbin' like turtle-doos,
They for my cope make siccar bed,
Brawn to my heart infuse.
Scant pinnin' you will here perceive—
The Greenhorn's 'Fail-me-never',
Frae foun' to crown I'm built to leeve,
Wi' aul' Time laith to sever.

For mony a mile o'er hechts and howes
My brither dykes extend,
Alike for gimmers, hoggs and yowes,
And stirks a shair godsend.
When winter's gales blaw lood and snell
They ken a siccar biel'
Frae summer's heat prolonged and fell
A cooling shade as weel.

It's lock and bind, and bind and lock,
    That's where the true skill lies,
Hence stand I firm as ony rock
    'Neath fair or frownin' skies.
Mute evidence nane can gainsay
    O' stalwarts lang syne gane,
Whose matchless worth frae day to day
    Still breathes frae ilka stane.

For shame ye mensless gomerils
    On selfish pleasure bent,
Who, heedless o' the crime it spells,
    The wanton devilment,
That ye win o'er my cope wi' speed,
    Rive aff fu' mony a stane,
Wi' ne'er the gumption in your heid
    To put it back again.

Say, dae ye never stop to think
    What wrang ye dae to men
Wha forged sae glorious a link
    In Dyke-Craft's gowden chain.
That he wad strive thus to undo
    Their wark that smiles at Age,
To a' braid Galloway and YOU
    A priceless Heritage?

A weel-built dyke's a bonnie sicht
    For ilka body's e'e,
A source o' keen and rare delicht
    Wherever it may be.
Whilst man may come and man may goe,
    Since life and man must sever,
If heed to our sma' needs ye pay
    We weel micht last forever.

Appendix 1

EARLY SURVEYS

The early surveys of counties in England, published by the Board of Agriculture, were compiled in the later years of the eighteenth century and in the early years of the nineteenth. The terms of reference were much the same as for Scotland, which has already been mentioned; later we will meet the similar surveys for Ireland.

The surveys for English counties were often compiled by the Chief Constables for each county. The observations of these writers were very cursory when they came to the chapter on Enclosures and dry stone walls. Considering the hundreds of miles of these erections which must have come under the heading of Enclosures they do not get the attention they deserve.

All that the survey of County Durham has to say is that its Enclosures date from the fifteenth century.

The Westmorland survey suggests that waste land should be enclosed by high stone walls and planted with larch. On Shap Fell those walls could be built 5½ feet high at 1/6 to 1/8 per rood of 7½ yards.

In Yorkshire East Riding on the Wolds, 'Turf Walls 4 or 5 feet high with a base of 3 to 4 feet and sometimes covered with a projecting sod, cost 1/- to 2/- per rood of 7 yards running measure'. This may include digging and carting.

In the North Riding Survey there is a good description of the method of laying a hedge. In the dales of North and West Ridings 'Stone walls without mortar are the prevailing fences. They are made without mortar about 5 feet high and generally coped with large stones laid horizontally or else with stones set on edge.'

Yorkshire West Riding. The only mention here of stone walls, is that of a farmer who ploughed deep and made a low wall of extracted stones 30 inches wide at the base. The next plough brought up more stones and so he raised the wall to the proper height.

The Estate Manager, by Henderson, tells us a good deal. He points out the merits of the Galloway hedge and states that the Galloway-dyke is best for sheep, but he does not say how the openwork top courses act as a deterrent. He considers unreclaimed moorland (he really means undrained land) unsuitable for dykes, but he should have added for other forms of fence too.

He points out that on irregular ground the cope would not follow the irregularity but should be 'toned down', that brittle stones should be left to weather, that stones abound in soils of oolitic formation and that there are 45 million acres of enclosed land in the United Kingdom.

It is a pity that his illustrations show two men building with the easiest of limestone rectangular blocks—child's play to a Galloway dyker—and he gives none of the finer points of the craft. Moreover the stones are being put in lengthways along the dyke and not across.

Apart from Henderson there is a very little information and even less instruction among these sources as to the principles and methods of building the many thousands of miles of stone walls that cover so much of the land. If it had not been that the Reverend Samuel Smith, the minister of the parish of Borgue in Kirkcudbrightshire, had a proper sense of the duties entrusted to him as the compiler of the Galloway Survey, we should not have had the craft properly explained.

It seems absurd that for any real instruction we should be dependent on a minister of the Scots Kirk who wrote in 1824. There are some 30 pages of the Galloway Survey devoted to dykes, whereas other compilers for other counties dismiss them in a paragraph. Scott (1885), in his book on farm architecture, gives an illustration of two dykers at work, but they are also using easy limestone blocks. They are putting them in sideways and the double looks hollow. Scott's illustration is exactly the same as Henderson's.

The Scottish surveys are better than those of England, but with the exception of that of Galloway by our reverend friend, they are of small importance, except as to the *galloway-dyke*. The same criticism applies to Ireland.

Appendix 2

GALLOWAY DYKES

'The upper courses of *galloway-dykes* ought to be made as narrow and open as possible, to afford the least footing for sheep and to let them see through. And if the first course of single stones should project a little over the double wall, so much the better. Of all dykes this is the most formidable for sheep. A double wall of twice the height will not turn them with equal certainty. The tottering appearance, and seeing light through the stones deter them from any attempt to scale it, together with the want of footing on top. These walls may be made of the coarsest stone, and when they are properly made, with the centre of gravity resting on the stones below, they stand better than double walls.'

The *Stirling Survey* says (1812):

'Of all the various sorts of fences now employed, the rudest and the simplest in its construction is the *galloway-dyke*. It is formed of large, ill-shaped stones, strongly wedged together for about two-thirds of its height, and then of stones gradually decreasing in size for 18 to 24 inches and more. The interstices between the stones are wide and the light showing through frightens the cattle, especially the sheep, and deters them from attempting them. They are cheaply erected and cheaply repaired. In the parishes of Fintry, Denny and St. Ninians, many miles of such dykes exist.'

The *Dumfriesshire Survey* (1812) says:

'The Galloway-Dyke is comparably the best, but a great deal of good and durable stone is necessary. It is never less than 5 feet high, often 5 feet 3 inches, being 32 inches broad at the grass, crosslaid with stones called throughbands, one for every 3 feet of length, and finished above with a series of long stones showing the light through the interstices and yet firmly holding by one another.'

The *Roxburgh Survey* (1798) says that dykes were often topped with turf, and that this is best done with the turves placed on edge and 'condensed together' with a spade. 'A few large stones placed loosely on the top above a kind of projecting cope, with apertures to admit light, deter both cattle and sheep from attempting to break through.' A footnote adds: 'Here called *galloway-dykes*, walls of that nature being common in Galloway.'

The *Hebrides Survey* says:

'The Galloway-Dyke, a species of enclosure commenced in 1720 in that Southern District of Scotland, and now well known and esteemed all over this kingdom, is the most advisable for the Western Isles. From 5 feet to 5 feet 10 inches in height, 3 feet thick at the bottom till within 18 inches of the top.' He goes on to say that the stones near the top afford daylight in the interstices of the stones and this terrifies sheep and cattle from any attempt to jump them.

Sinclair's *General Report* (1814) says:

'Though at first sight the open portion of this fence may appear slight, long experience has established its efficiency in deterring animals from climbing over, to a greater extent perhaps than a more solid wall of greater height. The solid part at bottom, at least 32 inches thick tapering to 18 inches, and 44 inches above the grass, the open work going 22 inches higher.'

Professor John Scott (1885) quotes from Sinclair.

Appendix 3

RUTHERFORD'S WITNESSES

Not far from Borgue, the parish of the Rev. Samuel Smith and of John McTaggart, lies the parish of Anwoth. Samuel Rutherford, a famous Scottish divine, was at one time minister of Anwoth. He is notable for much local lore. The well-known hymn 'The sands of time are sinking, the dawn of Heaven breaks', was written in his memory. Those words and the beautiful melody to which they have been set, have made and will continue to make a more lasting memorial in the minds of men than a sculptured tombstone. These latter, as time goes on to the fourth or fifth generation, begin to engender a slight though shamefaced feeling of irritation when signs of wear and incipient decay require attention and repairs which have somehow to be paid for.

In Rutherford's parish are two small clachans, Anwoth and Skyreburn, of half a dozen houses each, along the banks of two burns about a mile apart and separated by an intervening ridge. That strict Sabbatarian Rutherford learnt that the boys from these clachans used to meet on Sunday afternoons to play football. The venue was a flat piece of ground in a hollow near the top of the ridge. An admirable spot not easy to find and over ground rough enough to deter most interfering bodies.

But Rutherford was fairly roused and, accompanied by an elder, he strode off to this Sabbath-breaking scene. Sure enough, there they were and consternation reigned when the indignant Rutherford appeared. A rare dressing-down he gave them and the delinquents seemed duly abashed and, perhaps, repentant as he dismissed them to their homes.

He may have had misgivings as to the lasting effect of his admonitions, for he finished up by declaring that his conscience was clear and that he 'called these three stones to witness that he had done his duty'. These stones were three huge boulders, each as big as a chest of drawers. Ever since they have been called Rutherford's Witnesses.

There is a sequel to this improving tale.

A dyker, busy at work some years later, coveted one of these stones. He found that it could be cut up easily and could be used in his dyke. He declared that 'witness or no', that stone was to be used, and use it he did. His dyke, which is standing yet, runs about sixty yards down the slope. This amounted to something akin to sacrilege. The story goes that the dyker a few days later fell into a 'dwalm' from which he never really recovered. In plain English, he had a stroke. Another version is that a fishbone stuck in his throat. Whatever happened, it is quite certain that Rutherford's Witnesses are there still and likely so to remain, undisturbed and undesecrated. One is almost irresistibly reminded of the retribution that attended Fidgety Phil (who wouldn't sit still) and Johnny Head in Air. The reaction of most people is that it was jolly hard lines on an earnest industrious dyker.

INDEX